The **Honest** Life of a **Liar**

by Natalie Schweiger

DORRANCE PUBLISHING CO
EST. 1920
PITTSBURGH, PENNSYLVANIA 15238

The contents of this work, including, but not limited to, the accuracy of events, people, and places depicted; opinions expressed; permission to use previously published materials included; and any advice given or actions advocated are solely the responsibility of the author, who assumes all liability for said work and indemnifies the publisher against any claims stemming from publication of the work.

All Rights Reserved
Copyright © 2021 by Natalie Schweiger

No part of this book may be reproduced or transmitted, downloaded, distributed, reverse engineered, or stored in or introduced into any information storage and retrieval system, in any form or by any means, including photocopying and recording, whether electronic or mechanical, now known or hereinafter invented without permission in writing from the publisher.

Dorrance Publishing Co
585 Alpha Drive
Suite 103
Pittsburgh, PA 15238
Visit our website at www.dorrancebookstore.com

ISBN: 978-1-6470-2567-0
eISBN: 978-1-6470-2642-4

Special Acknowledgments To:

Michelle Schweiger
Because you are Mom, and your support is boundless.

EVERYBODY LIES. We humans do it every day, whether we're sugarcoating the consequence of a poor decision, making ourselves look better on a resume, trying to impress a protentional lover, or just fibbing you're sick so you can stay home and binge watch Netflix. (*Stranger Things*, anyone?) It's true. Everybody does it; if you disagree, you're just lying to yourself (Unless you're Ella from *Ella Enchanted*, in which case you physically cannot tell a lie. If so, I'm sorry, but thank you for reading my book.) Why do we, though? Because we don't like truth, whatever it happens to be. We say what we think people want to hear, what society says is politically correct. Well, to be frank, most politicians stress me out, and I'm done caring what people think. We're all the authors of our own story; why be ashamed to tell it how it is? My name is Natalie (but I guess you already know that from the cover). Have a seat, friend, doesn't matter if you're outside, inside, on a plane, in a car, kicked back on the couch, wherever you may be. Let's be honest for a while. This is my story.

~ ... ~ ... ~

Chapter 1
About New Places

"How are you liking everything?" the waitress asked, her forest-green apron swept the floor as she turned to refill my coffee mug.

"Great," I replied. "The toast is excellent."

"Why thank you. We make all our bread in-house," said the waitress.

"Well, I can tell." She smiled at me and I smiled back, then continued to make her rounds to the other tables. I looked up from my coffee, out the window of the café to the other side of Broadway Street, where many colorful false storefronts, ranging from art galleries to ice cream parlors made up the hub of the town. But the true beauty of this place lies behind all those shops.

Towering snowcapped coastal mountains, close enough to walk to, form a natural protective wall around Skagway, Alaska. This will be my home for the next five months, a new place full of new people and new adventures. But my story begins about two years prior. Allow me to take you back to October of 2016 where I was sitting at another table, looking out a different window, in a different state, getting ready to embark on yet another new journey.

~...~...~

"Gosh, I hope she picks up," I thought out loud to myself as I listened to the dial tone beep on my phone. A lukewarm cup of coffee rested by my elbow, on the table scattered with addresses and classified ads. My foot tapped impatiently. I had been apartment searching for the past week and was coming up empty with each attempt. Either the place was too small, the rent was too much, the apartment already sold, or sometimes the landlord just never answered. That's classifieds for you. But this time I was feeling very confident. I looked out the kitchen window on to the covered swimming pool and pondered why I was looking for an apartment in Colorado in the first place....

~...~...~

My boyfriend Trevor and I had been dating for almost a year at this point, and from the day we met I knew he had plans to move out of southern Illinois and go West. The location however wasn't set in stone. We talked about it all the time: how we were going to kick off the dust of this small town and follow our dreams. We both have adventurous spirits, sharing a love of anything outdoors, going on spontaneous hiking trips where the end destination wasn't decided until we got there. Most people of our generation, I thought, shared that same longing of traveling beyond their area code. Every twenty-one-year-old with a fresh associates degree says they're moving away to satisfy that restless hunger. Trevor and I were no exception, but what set us apart from many of our friends and family is that we were going to do it.

A month before this phone call, I was working as a chef on a cruise ship in Hawaii, (that story will be in the next book) and doing some job hunting for after my contract ended, when I saw an opening for sous chef at Winter Park Resort in Winter Park Colorado. Trevor had talked of going on ski trips there in the past, and how much he loved it. I had never been to Colorado other than passing through. Sous chef would be like jumping three steps in my career, but I lived for new opportunities and always invited new challenges.

What the hell, I thought. Within forty minutes I had filled out all the application questions, attached my resume and clicked submit. A week later I had the job.

"Well, we look forward to seeing you in November!" my soon-to-be manager said over the phone. Elated and somewhat in disbelief, I thought, *Wow, guess I'm going to Colorado*. The following thought was, *We're going to need a place to live*.

Mid-ring a voice came over the phone, snapping me back from my daydream.

"Hello, this is Peggy."

"Oh, Hey Peggy this is Natalie, I'm calling about the apartment you had for sale online...."

We talked for half an hour, and by the end of the conversation, she seemed very interested in Trevor and I becoming potential tenants. To seal the deal, though, she wanted to meet us in person and give us a tour. At this point I was getting desperate for a place to live, so I immediately called Trevor and we prepared for a last-minute trip to Winter Park.

That weekend we loaded up the rental car. With Trevor, my mom, my younger brother Jonathan and I settled in, we set off on the thirteen-hour drive.

~…~…~

If you've ever driven from the Midwest to Colorado, you'll know that you must drive through Kansas. Which is pretty much eight hours of corn fields, wheat fields, cow pastures, and the occasional tumbleweed. The only break from this perpetual flatland is when you reach the acres of windmills, but even those giant powerhouses lose their thrill after the second gas station stop. So, when the Rocky Mountains finally make their appearance on the horizon, there's nothing like it. Driving over that last hill as the sun is setting and seeing those peaks glow in the distance after being on the road for ten hours, is absolutely beautiful.

~…~…~

I had driven through the mountains back when Trevor and I made a trip out to Yosemite National Park, but still it was a surreal feeling to watch them rise higher the closer we got. Like a giant soldier under Momma Nature's command, they stood resolute before the fading sunlight. Their raw size and strength were a little daunting, not just asking, but commanding respect from every being they encountered. At the same time, the mountains offer a sense of security, a Safe Haven against the elements. Just like any living thing, if you treat it with kindness, you'll see all the beauty and wonder they can offer. During that drive through the Rockies, I couldn't pull my gaze away from the window. To any passing car I'm sure I looked like a kid at a candy shop storefront.

As we passed through Denver, over Berthoud Pass, and into the town of Winter Park, those mountains spoke to me. They held out their hands to pull me into this Valley town. Even though the streets were new, and the people walking them were all strangers, something about this place said welcome home.

Following the directions from the GPS, we drove out of town, up a winding road into a small subdivision lined with two-story log cabins. Unlike the communities back in Illinois, where every house seemed to be built after one of three cookie-cutter blueprints, these homes were individually unique. This gave the place a sense of originality.

Soon the friendly robot voice chirped "you have reached your destination" and we pulled into the driveway of a quaint, two-story home where a woman I assumed to be Peggy stood waiting. We stepped out of the car, and she reached her hand out to formally introduce us to herself and her home. She was tall and thin, with a quiet voice and a big smile.

"Welcome to Colorado!" she said, gesturing for us to follow. "I hope your drive wasn't too bad."

"No not at all." I smiled back "We've been looking forward to seeing the apartment."

"Well, come on then, let me give you the grand tour." Peggy walked under an overhang that doubled as the floor to the second story balcony and turned the key to the door leading into a basement apartment. I had never looked for an apartment, but I had been to friends' and seen college dorms, so I had a sense of what was worth the money and what was not. This place was well worth it. As soon as I walked in the door, a lovely furnished living room set off to the right, complete with a long couch, love seat, and gas fireplace in the corner. Just behind the living room was a decent-size kitchen space, with a full refrigerator and dishwasher. Separating the kitchen from the living room was an eight-foot-long countertop with plenty of working room. Directly in front of me was the door to a master bedroom, to my left a full bathroom. It had everything we needed. The best part was, adjacent to the living area, a walkout sunroom with a sliding glass door separating it from the rest of the basement. Its tall windows let in rays of sunlight, which fell on two potted trees sitting on a stone floor. A wooden rocking chair was draped with a red Afghan set in the corner, and I could already see myself sitting there on a winter morning, sipping coffee while the snow fell outside.

I turned to Trevor and saw he was feeling the same way about this apartment. I tried not to let my immediate excitement slip into my expression, but I've never mastered a great poker face. Peggy asked more questions than we did. But after a full tour and discussion of lease agreements we had agreed to take the apartment. Peggy thanked us for coming out, with the promise of sending a copy of the signed agreement via email the next day. My mom and Jonathan were staying at the Holiday Inn that night, but Trevor and I wanted to camp, so, we headed out to the campsite first. On the way I kept getting more and more elated. Other than buying my car, this was the first real grown-up thing I had ever done. I was feeling so tremendously accomplished, like I had just won the grand prize on *The Price Is Right*. Trevor too was very happy, and relieved that we had finally found a good place to stay. My mother, on the other hand, was not so enthused. She's the kind of woman who, no matter how she feels about a situation, always has something to say. The entire drive to the campground she didn't say a single word. Her face held a blank expression and her knuckles were white from such a firm grip on the steering wheel.

Oh no, I thought. *She's mad about something, like really seriously bothered.*

Well, that realization knocked my good vibes down a few levels. I could sense a lecture coming on. It was bound to happen. Then, as we pulled into our campsite at Lake Granby, I fell from Cloud 9 back to reality.

~…~…~

My mother and I had always had a great relationship, sure we had our moments, no different, though, from the usual parent-child arguments (which I typically lost, but 90 percent of the time we got along swimmingly). Whether it was how much flour to add to a cookie dough recipe or figuring out if this guy is really worth it, I could go to her for any kind of advice. As I got older, we grew even closer, and I started to realize just how much we had in common. I would confidently tell anyone that my mom was my best friend.

I thought the success of the day would make her feel as happy as I did. Well, I was wrong; they say that the stronger your love is for someone the greater the pain when they hurt you.

Of course, I would never intentionally try to hurt my mom, but the thought hadn't occurred to me how all this was affecting her. To me, moving out and trying this life thing on my own, was an exciting adventure, but for my mom, it was quite the opposite. I wasn't (and still am not) a parent, so I didn't know what it felt like to see my child grow up and leave home. I'm told in most cases it isn't easy. How could I have neglected to think about this. Of course, she would be upset.

Now a twinge of guilt crept over me as we set up our tent and started gathering firewood.

I should go and talk to her, I thought.

But when I turned to look for her, she was gone. The campsite wasn't big, so I knew she couldn't have gone far. Leaving Jonathan and Trevor to tend the fire, I set off down the road to find my mother. Soon enough, I spotted a figure with their hood up, hands in their pockets and walking very briskly toward the entrance of the campsite.

"Mom!" I called out. The figure stopped but wouldn't turn around.

Great, I thought, *so she's not even going to look at me.*

I jogged over and stopped, slightly winded, at her side

"Why did you leave? What's wrong?" I asked. She took a moment to respond, but finally said, "I don't like this, Natalie. I don't like this at all."

"What do you mean? I thought today went great. What don't you like?" I pleaded.

"Everything!" she shouted. "I don't think you should have agreed to that apartment so soon, and I have a really bad feeling about those people. I don't think you really know what you're doing, and I am worried about you guys making it out here on your own."

I could tell she was holding back tears. The one thing I hated most was seeing my mom cry. Taking in what she said I chose my words carefully.

"Well… I'm sorry you feel this way. I wasn't trying to hurt your feelings, but I think this is a good move for us. I mean… yeah, we're going to make some mistakes, but that's how we learn, right? You said so yourself; you don't want me living at home forever. Plus, I've never had any problem providing for myself, you know how I value independence."

I was trying to reassure her, but she just kept her gaze straight ahead. After a pregnant pause she said, "I know you are independent, but it's not you I'm worried about. I'm so afraid you will have to pick up the slack from someone else. I just don't want anything or anyone dragging you down."

Ah there it is. This was the real reason she was so upset.

My parents had never shown any dislike towards Trevor. My dad pulled him aside one evening to tell him how glad he was to see me with someone who really made me happy. He had never come close to saying something like that to any previous boyfriends of mine. I thought Mom liked him too. They always were laughing when we went out together and enjoyed the time we spent with family. But then again, we still were living at home. No matter how late we stayed out, I would go back to my parents' house, and Trevor would go back to his. We had only spent the night together a few times, and those were only because circumstances made it unsafe to drive, or we were on a camping trip with friends. Now we would not only be living in the same house, sharing the same bed, but our parents were 900 miles away. This was difficult for my mother to process. My family raised me in a Catholic home where living together was not appropriate until after marriage. As an adolescent I agreed with The Church completely. That is until I started dating, fell in love, and found someone I wanted to share my life with.

It's funny how as a child, I thought my parents' views on the world were 100 percent correct. Then, once I was in situations where those beliefs were tested. I began questioning them, and my way of thinking started to change. In recent years, this had made for an uncomfortable situation. I was in one now, stuck between a rock and a hard place, not wanting to offend my mother, but needing to tell her the truth of how I felt.

My parents didn't know Trevor the way that I did. They only saw the fun-loving, adventures boy, who enjoyed challenging his friends, and who tended to be reckless. This is fine if the goal is to simply have a good time. But we were about to take a big step into our young adulthood. This decision required patience, organization, compromise and a lot of maturity my parents thought Trevor lacked. They knew I could take care of myself, but if I was going to be living with another, they wanted reassurance that I could rely on that person too.

Yes, Trevor was a bit on the spontaneous side. He didn't have a lot of experience in saving money, and his priorities weren't always in a responsible order. But hasn't everybody been at this point in their life? Some just had to grow up faster than others.

Trevor was fortunate to be raised in a family that had the means to support all of his hobbies and interests, giving him and his younger brother a beautiful home and environment to grow up in. This allowed him to not have to worry about money very often. Now don't get the wrong idea; he wasn't spoiled by any means. His parents instilled in him a good work ethic, what it means to earn your rewards and the importance of respecting your peers.

These were some of the qualities I saw in him every day. When I looked at him, I saw a guy who, no matter the job, would work the hardest of all his coworkers, never stopping until it was done properly. I saw a guy who loved life and everything it had to offer. His personality paralleled mine in the way he always had a positive outlook. He saw the good in everyone regardless of what others said about them. True, he had his flaws, but no human being is perfect. There are so many things I loved about Trevor, but his best trait was his loyalty and commitment.

As a couple, we got along with just about anyone, and when it came to close friends, we each had a handful of people we could go to for anything, and I like to think those friends felt the same about us. When Trevor made a bond with someone, it was close to unbreakable. He followed through on his word. So, if he said he'll be there for someone, he will. If he says he's sorry, he really is, and if he says I love you, he means it with all his heart.

All these things made my decision to move in with him a no-brainer. I didn't know entirely what to expect after moving out, but I did know I could trust Trevor, and the easiest way to get my mom onboard with the idea, was to use her trust in me.

I told her that day, there on the campsite road, that if she could please just trust my trust in him, that everything would work out all right. Besides, if worst came to worst, we would each have a place to come back to.

That seemed to help a little. I knew she still wasn't thrilled, but her demeanor brightened a bit. We walked back down to the tent were Trevor and Jonathan had a warm fire, waiting to cook a delicious outdoor dinner

~...~...~

Chapter 2
About Moving

Standing in the doorway of my old bedroom, I wondered when the next time would be, I would sleep in it. The room was unnaturally clean, and I marveled at how much space was there. *Oh well*, I thought, *no time for reminiscing.*

I bent down, and with a grunt, lugged the massive duffel bag containing every piece of clothing I owned (minus a few old school uniforms and prom dresses I left hanging in the closet) down the hall through the kitchen and into my little SCION FR-S waiting in the garage. I was pleasantly surprised at how much she (the SCION) could hold. My back windshield was completely covered, save a small five-inch by four-inch square at the top. Packed to the brim, I was finally ready to go. Saying goodbye to my parents wasn't as hard as I thought it would be. My mom cried a little, but I was too excited to be sad. With one last "I love you, be safe, call us when you get there," I was off. Out again on that long drive West to Colorado where my new home awaited.

You may be wondering, "where was Trevor?" Well, because he was still in school and the semester didn't end until December 12. I had two weeks by myself in the apartment. Which was fine. I thought it would give me a chance to set it up and have it looking nice and homey by the time Trevor got there.

Driving was something that had always come naturally. I had never gotten anxious in traffic, worried about the road conditions, or stressed over long drives. I had been looking forward to this trip for the last month. Weather was uneventful through Kansas and smooth sailing in the Front Range of Colorado. So, when I saw a few snow flurries bounce off my windshield passing through Denver, I didn't think anything of it. I had driven through snow before. Besides it wasn't covering the road yet, how bad could it be?

This was my first false assumption. Oh, how wrong I was. Little did I know that the weather in Colorado can go 0-100 in a matter of minutes, especially over a mountain pass. In a short amount of time those cute little flurries had turned into angry ice pellets, blowing sideways against my car, covering the road in a sheet of snow and freezing in clumps on my windshield wipers. I looked out at the white lines marking the shoulder. This became my only way of knowing where the road ended. Barely being able to see fifteen feet in front of me, my speed slowed to twenty-five miles an hour. Then the highway started to climb. If you know anything about cars, you'll know it's ideal to have all-wheel or at least front-wheel drive in such conditions. I had neither. This fun zippy sports car was great on freeways in the summer, but my rear-wheel drive orientation turned her from a stallion to a drunk pony.

I was down to fifteen miles an hour, creeping gingerly around every switchback, praying that each turn would be the last one before town. With the storm continuing to blow snow in all directions, every tap to the gas pedal had me fishtailing. Going downhill it didn't matter how gently I feathered the brakes; my wheels would spin, and my heart pounded faster. At one point I was completely sideways and came to a dead stop in the middle of Highway 40. There I thought of just waiting until the morning. My anxiety was higher than it had ever been in my life, but if the blizzard kept up, I might really get stuck. So, I took a breath, said a prayer, and pressed on down the mountain pass, white knuckled and wide eyed. After what felt like a lifetime, I saw the glow of a streetlight in the distance, still foggy and blurred against the swirling snow. Then another appeared, and another until finally the sign reading Welcome to Winter Park passed by my windshield. I let out a holler of crazed relief that I had made it over the mountain. Now I just needed to get to the apartment in one piece.

~...~...~

Although I was done with the sharp curves and steep hills, I still had one last climb before I could relax. The apartment was up behind the town on a road that wasn't yet plowed. Thankfully it was wider than the highway, so when I did slide sideways (which I did) there was more room for recovery. At long last I saw the apartment, and in my relief accidentally stomped on the gas, lurching the car forward.

"Oh Jesus," I said.

Reflexively I then slammed on the brakes, which of course didn't stop the car but sent it skidding into the ditch at the foot of the driveway, nose in the snow butt in the air.

"Shit."

Well at least I made it, I thought. This probably wasn't where they wanted me to park, but I'd rather be stuck in a snowy ditch outside my living room window than somewhere on Highway 40. I was too stressed to think about it now. Besides it was late and very very cold. *I'll deal with this in the morning.*

Reaching back, I grabbed my backpack containing essentials for one night, dredged up the driveway and into the basement apartment that was thankfully unlocked. Then collapsed onto the couch, exhausted. All I wanted was a strong drink followed by a sound sleep. A friend had sent me with some Makers Mark whiskey, so I opened the bottle and made myself a Manhattan, drank it in a matter of minutes, then promptly fell asleep on the couch.

What a night.

~…~…~

The next morning, I woke up to the worst hangover. Because of the stress from the previous night, I hadn't considered how the altitude would affect alcohol consumption. Not to mention, I didn't have any kind of dinner and the lack of hydration wasn't helping either.

So, there I was with a pounding headache, a dry mouth, and a nauseated stomach on my first morning in Colorado. I had barely sat up when there was a soft knock on the door.

"Good morning, Natalie! Are you awake?" came a voice from outside.

"Yes, I'm up." I sounded like I had been chain-smoking all night.

It was Vernon, here to help me with my car. The pounding in my temple had made me temporarily forget I had left it in the ditch outside. I got dressed as quick as I could and tried to look not half-dead as I walked out to help. With Vernon's pickup truck and tow rope, my car rolled out of the ditch easily, but it took more effort, and half an hour of pushing and pulling to get it halfway up the driveway. With the steep incline and slick snow, this was as far as the SCION was going. I thanked him tremendously, and he wished me a happy first day in the apartment. Not exactly how I was planning this day to go, but I guess it could only get better from here. Stuff could wait to be unloaded until later, I now desperately wanted a glass of water and a hot cup of coffee. Luckily Peggy had left A bag of Ground Dark Roast on the table as a welcoming gift.

After I was hydrated, the headache subsided slightly, but I was still nowhere ready to greet the day. So, I chose to curl up on the couch with my hot coffee mug held against the side of my head, and eventually fall asleep to the Food Network until this hangover had run its course.

The next few days passed much easier than the first. With my things unpacked, room arranged, and car in an actual parking spot, the little basement was starting to feel very cozy. Vernon and Peggy were kind and very helpful while I adjusted to mountain life. Until Trevor arrived, they let my use their spare vehicle so I could safely drive back and forth to town and to work.

My orientation was three days post-arrival. Winter Park Resort had a unique work environment, unlike any other place I had cooked for. There were many food establishments at the resort; mine was The Jane Café. It was just me and seven other employees running breakfast and lunch for the flocks of skiers. Everyone was super laid-back and easygoing. We all quickly became friends, and even though I was still learning how to run this kitchen, my afternoons passed without much difficulty.

December, though, is not peak ski season. Many high priority days were sure to come, but at this point the snow base was only at eighteen inches, not enough to open the entire resort. But when the snow did finally fall, it fell for days. Oh, how I will never forget seeing (not driving through) that first Colorado Blizzard.

I woke up to my alarm flashing and beeping. In the robotic monotone voice, it chirped "It's 7:30 A.M. Time to get up"

I swung my feet around to the floor and glancing at the window I noticed it seemed a bit darker and oddly quiet. I reached up to pull back the curtains and saw it was completely covered in white.

Oh my gosh, I thought. *It snowed overnight.*

Did it ever, I ran into the living room, opened the sunroom door to the largest window the basement had, and looked outside to see a blanket of white covering everything in the neighborhood. I felt the rush of excitement I used to feel as a fourth grader when there was a snow day. Hurriedly I gulped down a bowl of cereal, scalded the roof of my mouth with the coffee I drank too fast, put on my layers of jackets and socks, slipped into my boots, and was out the door. The air was crisp and so very cold, but in the wake of the storm, there wasn't the slightest hint of a breeze. The road had not yet been plowed, so it looked as though I was in a far-off cabin in the mountains, hidden from the bustle of civilization. I knew the town of Winter Park was only six minutes down the road, but I pretended that it wasn't. My imagination was on a level it hadn't been on in a long time. With a good whoop, I scooped up a handful of snow and threw it into the air, letting the crystals float back down to land on my face like soft icy kisses.

What a lovely sensation, I thought.

But this was only the front yard. I had so much more to explore. Happily, I turned and plowed my way up the hill into the grove of Aspen trees behind the house. Small woodland footprints dotted the snow around the base of the trees, leaving a playful trail from their many morning outings. To my right, a rabbit hopped from bush to bush. His soft nose quivering after each leap in search of breakfast. Overhead a falcon soared ever so silently; if it wasn't for his shadow cast on the ground, I wouldn't have thought to look up.

Wow. These animals were carrying about their business as they did every day, not appearing to be phased by the three feet of snow covering their burrows and dens. Meanwhile, I was so in awe of the new landscape, I didn't know where to look next.

In most heavily populated areas, snow means a day spent inside. People retreat to the warmth of their temperature-controlled houses. Only stepping outside if necessary. Yes, for many the cold means hibernation. Afterall, the plants lose their leaves, color subsides, and creeks freeze into silence. Any passerby in search of warmth sees Momma Nature as lifeless. But here she was very much alive.

The snow covered any blemish on the ground and the road. It filled in holes and smoothed over any sharp rocks or fallen limbs. The mountains, which yesterday only had a dusting blowing about their peaks, now were nearly completely covered to the base in a heavy white blanket. They appeared larger yet less rugged. Kind of like a weathered farmer in his Sunday best, slowly rocking back and forth on the porch swing, eyes closed letting the sun warm his face after a long week's hard work.

Spruce and aspens rose up from the drifts below the tree line in long rows, creating wooded trails down to the bottom. It was postcard perfect, and as far as I knew, mine were the only human eyes to see it. Taking a deep breath, I continued through the Grove to the road. The snow wasn't as deep here, so my steps came quicker and easier. I walked for about a mile stopping frequently to take pictures to send back home. I wished that my friends could see this. I missed them. I missed Trevor. He would love this just as much as I did. But in five more days he would be here, and then we could play in the snow together.

I hadn't texted him yet that morning. The fresh snowfall had wiped anything else from my mind, but my fingers were starting to go numb from the cold, so I made my way back to the house. Running downhill in knee deep powder can be quite challenging. I fell multiple times, and on the fourth tumble landed face-first, nose in a bush (you may be thinking I should have just walked instead of trying to run. That would have made sense, wouldn't it? Well I do a lot of things that don't make sense. Stop judging.)

For whatever reason, maybe the shock from the cold or just the silliness of my predicament, I started laughing, and laughed and laughed until tears were rolling down my rosy cheeks. Flipping onto my back I did the best I could to make a snow angel. Then, laying there surrounded by all that fresh powder, I sighed and thought, *I think this will be a good winter.*

The next four days moved about as fast as a Hawthorn Tree. (Hawthorns are one of the slowest growing trees out there, look it up.) On the fifth day, I woke up at 5:00 A.M. and couldn't go back to sleep. Trevor was finally arriving today. I was so excited I couldn't sit still for more than ten minutes at a time. I was constantly finding little chores to keep myself busy. He was texting me updates throughout the morning on his progress. The roads were a bit icy that night, but he had a vehicle suitable for such conditions, so I wasn't worried. At 10:55 P.M., I perched myself on the arm of the couch and just waited. I couldn't keep focus long enough to complete a task, and the apartment by now was spotless. When I saw headlights down the driveway, I leapt from the couch to peep out the window, and there he was. I ran to the door, allowed him two steps inside before tackling him in a bear hug. The frigid air blew in from the open door, but it didn't matter. My guy was back safe and sound, I forgot all about the waiting, any anxiety disappeared. Trevor was here, and it finally felt like home.

~...~...~

Chapter 3
About Presents

The next few weeks flew by. I helped Trevor get moved in. He started his job working as a lift operator for Winter Park, business picked up for me as well at The Jane Café. With the approaching holidays and continuing snowfall, people from all over Colorado, Texas, California, Kansas, everywhere, came flocking to the resort for their winter breaks and family vacations. Busy holidays were nothing new for me, though. Anyone in the culinary world will laugh in your face if you ask off for Christmas. So, I wasn't shocked when I learned I would be working December 19 through the 31. My only concern was when Trevor and I could celebrate ourselves. He knew my schedule was out of my hands and had no problem with this year's Christmas being a little less than traditional. We both were good when it came to compromise and planning around each other's busy work weeks, as long as we got a moment to pause and enjoy the holiday.

But before I got to Christmas, I must take into consideration that December was also my birthday month—the twentieth to be exact. As previously mentioned, Trevor wasn't great yet with money, and I knew this. So, the morning of my birthday I wasn't expecting much, and that was fine. He gave me a card and made me blueberry pancakes for breakfast, but when there was no present, I think he was the one who felt disappointed.

Trevor is an excellent gift giver and takes pride in thinking and planning what the receiver will like best. He always makes them very meaningful, and usually useful too. I knew he was low on funds, but this showed me just how low. Looking at him from across the table he was moving his pancake around the syrup puddle on his plate and staring glumly into his coffee.

"Hey," I said, reaching to grab his hand. "What's up?"

He set his fork down, leaned back in the chair and twiddled with the tablecloth.

"I'm sorry I don't have a present for you on your birthday.... I'm a bad boyfriend," he murmured into his lap.

This made me chuckle.

"No. No you are not." I smiled and made him look at me.

"Listen, I don't need a gift to be happy on my birthday. I told you, you didn't have to get me anything this year." Which was true. I had told him that to relieve some of the pressure, but still half expected something small. I could see how bothered he was though, and quickly pushed the selfish thought from my mind.

"Look." I told him firmly. "I would rather have no present from a broke boyfriend who really cares, then some useless materialistic knickknack from a boyfriend who thinks price tags are all girls pay attention too." And I truly meant that. Trevor knew I did too, and his mood lifted a little. He kissed my forehead and told me I was too good for him. But his pancakes quickly disappeared after that.

~...~...~

Later that week, December 23 (speaking of presents) I was in the bedroom with the door locked wrapping his Christmas gifts. (I know it's last minute, but don't tell me you've never done this before.) Trevor had just walked in and knocked on the door to see what I was up to. When I shouted back that I was wrapping his gift, he got very quiet. Usually he would have some witty response as to why he should be able to come in and sneak a peek at his present. It wasn't like him. So, I shoved everything under the bed and walked out to see him sitting against the back of the couch, looking just like he did the morning of my birthday.

Oh, dear, I thought.

I went to join him on the floor, and before I could speak, he said, "You shouldn't have gotten me anything."

"Come on, don't be silly. Of course, I was going to get you a Christmas present," I told him.

"Well, I feel really bad, then, because I don't have anything for you."

This I didn't expect. The birthday, yes. But no Christmas gift threw me off a bit. I guess he was struggling financially more than I realized. Maybe it was a pride thing for him, but I had never been in a situation where I couldn't afford a single Christmas gift, so I didn't understand completely where he was coming from. Remember, I have no poker face. My expression always says exactly what I am thinking. So, I was sure my look only squashed his pride even more. This was the first time in our relationship we had a serious talk about money.

Moving from the floor to the couch, I asked him why he was so short on funds, and more importantly why didn't he tell me.

He confessed he didn't want me to think he couldn't take care of himself, or that he was being irresponsible or lazy. Which I understood, no one wants to show signs of weakness to their significant other; it's a hard thing to do, especially after such big life changes. He felt like he was falling behind instead of moving forward.

He told my how he had never had money saved and the little he did before the move was quickly taken by rent, gas, and food. Working lift operations doesn't make a killing, so now he was living (unknown to me until now) paycheck to paycheck. I sighed, a little disappointed that he hadn't told me sooner, but I assured him I didn't care about the lack of presents under the tree. I already had a box from family waiting to be opened, plus if he was really beating himself up about it there would be more Christmases.

"Well you can make up for this one next year." I joked, nudging him with my shoulder. He smiled and gave me a hug.

"I'm sorry I'm a bad boyfriend," he said for the second time now that week.

"Stop that," I retorted, holding my hand up. "I don't want to hear you say that again. You are NOT a bad boyfriend, and tomorrow night we will have a great Christmas Eve. No sad faces, okay?"

"Fine," he said. But he was laughing now, and as I got up to finish wrapping, he pulled me back onto the couch where an intense tickling match ensued until both our sides hurt from laughing. Catching my breath, now back on the floor, I remembered I had a bottle of rosé in the fridge.

"Hey," I said, brushing a few strands of hair out of my face. "Want to watch a movie after I finish wrapping."

"I would love that," he replied.

"Okay great, you pick one out and pour me a glass of wine, I'll be back in fifteen minutes."

~ ... ~ ... ~

The following evening, Christmas Eve. We came home from work to have our first holiday away from home. For Trevor's family, it was tradition to make clam chowder for Christmas Eve dinner. So, we continued that here up in Colorado, and around 9:30 P.M., we sat down to hot soup, a delicious spinach salad with homemade dressing (made by yours truly, of course) and a bottle of champagne. There wasn't a Christmas tree surrounded by gifts, or a table festively decorated with candles and poinsettias, but we did have a cozy apartment and a crackling fireplace to sit next to. That warm fuzzy Christmas feeling was still there. Which if you take out all the hustle and bustle, is what really matters. Trevor and I took turns opening gifts our family had sent us. Overall, it was a great evening. We talked about Christmas back home and laughed at the retelling of timeless family stories that get told every year. Once the kitchen was cleaned up and wrapping paper gathered away, we sat down on the couch to watch *The Muppets Christmas Carol*. This was one of my family traditions.

Cuddled up there on the couch, I smiled at our little home. It really made me reconsider my priorities and expectations for the holiday season. We didn't have much, but we had genuine love for each other. (I know that sounds super cliché, but isn't that what Christmas is really about?)

If you've ever seen *A Charlie Brown Christmas*, (which if you haven't, stop reading right now and go watch it. It doesn't matter if you don't celebrate Christmas. It's a movie that can warm the hearts of many, even the Scrooges of the world.) In the end, Linus is comforting his friends by quoting Luke 2:8-14, and ends his message with "Glory to God in the highest, and on earth Peace, good will toward men. That's what Christmas is all about, Charlie Brown."

Just something to think about next time you're feeling less than appreciative on December 24.

As the movie played, I laid my head down on the pillow in Trevor's lap. He leaned over to kiss the top of my head and then softy whispered, "I love you."

"I love you too," I whispered back.

Then, with a sigh of contentment, I drifted off to sleep.

~ ... ~ ... ~

Chapter 4

About Rain and Snow (aka trying to ski)

As expected, life with the resort only got busier. My overtime hours grew longer, and time spent at the apartment was mostly just for decompression and sleep. Our days off didn't match up, so we would go for quite a while where the only time we would see each other was in front of the TV after a long day, with a drink in one hand and a phone in the other. I know Facebook, Instagram, and Snapchat shouldn't be a distraction when your significant other is sitting ten feet away from you. But society couldn't refer to us as millennials if we didn't live up to a few stereotypes.

Honestly, though, you can't be reading this book and tell me you aren't guilty of this too.

Anyway, as you can imagine, with such conflicting schedules, and lack of good conversation, we began to disconnect. Not in a sense that we stopped liking each other. But we just fell into a routine that didn't involve time for each other or real communication. It was the first stagnant point we had ever reached in our relationship. And just like water when it remains still for too long, unwanted things will start to grow. Small nonissues, such as clothes on the floor or dishes in the sink, would cause an argument. Instead of thinking of the other person's feelings, we both started to act more selfish, and nitpicky. I noticed myself pointing out things Trevor forgot, and using his insecurities to guilt him into doing certain chores, or so I could win an argument. We became very critical of each other and started acting more like siblings then boyfriend and girlfriend. There was always a slight tension in the air neither of was wanted to break. Because that would mean the other would win. Win what? I don't know; bragging rights?

I accused him of not caring enough, and he came back with I was too sensitive. Many small inconveniences would raise the tension, but the one thing above all that got to me was Trevor skiing.

As a Lifty (Mountain speak for lift operator) Trevor basically got paid to help people on the chairs and got an hour ride break. There were some days when the crowds would diminish and the lifties took turns playing on the Mountain. Trevor had been skiing since he was a little boy. Over the years and especially in the past two months he had gotten quite good. He loved the sport, and was always talking about it, like it was the only thing he could think about.

At first it didn't bother me, but after a while I became annoyed *Oh my gosh, can he talk about anything else?!* I would think to myself. I couldn't relate at all because not only had I not been out on the mountain yet, but I had never even put on a pair of skis in my life. I had new shiny ski boots with a pair of used Twin Tips in the corner waiting for me to break them in. But I didn't have the slightest idea where to start. It didn't help the case that Trevor seemed to have no interest in helping me learn. All he would say was "When are you going to take these skis out?" or "Are you ever going to use these on an actual mountain?"

Yes, of course I wanted to try, but just like you can't simply hand a sixteen-year-old with no manual driving experience the keys to a stick shift, and expect them to have a smooth ride all the way home, you can't send someone who has never skied before up the mountain and expect them to have a good time. (unless you're a jackass and enjoy watching your friends fail miserably, which, believe me, I know a few who this was their first skiing experience.)

But the more he talked about how great the snow was or how awesome a tree run he had that afternoon, the more jealous and determined I became. Initially I wanted my first time out to be with him, but at this point I didn't care anymore. My next day off, I was going skiing. One of my coworkers, as well as neighbors had the same day off as me, so they agreed that following Thursday to make a day of it. This friend was a snowboarder but still a beginner, so he had no problem sticking to the easy green slopes.

I'd like to take a moment to properly introduce this fellow coworker. He worked as the sous chef in the restaurant on the main floor, directly below the Jane Café. We had to collaborate frequently with product shipping and shared ingredients, so I saw him many times throughout the day. But I will never forget the first time I met him. He walked through the doorway between the kitchen and the dining area wearing an unbuttoned chefs coat, a black T-shirt underneath, black jeans, and a flat bill flipped backwards on his head. Under his hat he had shaggy, sandy red hair streaked with amber highlights.

"Natalie, this is Rain," our food and beverage director had said to me. "You two will probably be working together a lot this winter"

Rain… hmm, I had thought. *What a cool name.*

He reached out to shake my hand, and I did the same. But when our eyes met, something happened. A familiar feeling suddenly washed over me, a sensation I had felt only three times prior to this, and each time it was when I met somebody who's life later became very closely interwoven with mine. It's difficult to explain, and maybe you can relate, or maybe you'll think I'm crazy, but it's like meeting someone and instantly knowing they will become very important to you. Like if you have a close call with death and your past flashes before your eyes, only instead you're doing something totally normal (like working) and when you see them, you see a flash of your future. This isn't me saying I'm a fortune teller, and this isn't "love and first sight." (admittedly, I did fall for two of the three people previously mentioned, but it was a gradual falling, not right away.) It's just some kind of intense intuition I've always had. And it happened again with Rain.

"Hey," I exhaled a little too loudly. "It's nice to meet you."

"Yea you too." He grinned.

I noticed his smile was a little crooked; his mouth pulled slightly more to the left. I liked that. With his other hand, he reached up to adjust dark-rimmed glasses that had slid down his nose. Perhaps it was the reflection of the light on his lenses, but behind them I couldn't tell if his eyes were brown or green.

After letting go of our handshake, we held a brief businesslike conversation with our food and beverage director, then went back to our mornings to-do list. Since then we had developed a very amicable employee friendship, nothing out of the ordinary.

Anyways, for now he was just the guy who agreed to help me ski. That morning I geared up, loaded my ski poles and boots in the Ford Escape and drove about 400 yards down the road to pick up Rain. Nervous and excited, we set off for the resort.

The trouble started before I'd even gotten to the lift line. Thankfully, Trevor had shown me which way the boots go into the bindings and how to click the heal in properly, but this was more difficult with the boots actually on my feet, and to be standing on real snow instead of our living room carpet. After trial and error, I finally got my skis clicked in and scooted and shuffled my way to the lift corral. Poor Rain had been ready and waiting for a while, but as a boarder I didn't expect his assistance in getting my gear on. Sitting on the lift, riding up to the top was one of the coolest things I had done in Colorado thus far. I will never forget turning around in my seat to see the resort and Valley grow smaller as we rose to the top. My excitement grew and nerves subsided as we neared the top but quickly returned when I realized I now had to get off of a moving lift. I watched the people in front of me stand up and slide down off the ramp with no trouble.

Oh, that's not so hard, I thought.

Well, I mimicked those ahead and stood up as the chair got to the top of the ramp, but immediately lost balance and fell to the ground popping off a ski in the process. The lift operator stopped the lift and helped me stand up. A little embarrassed, I shuffled over to a flat spot with Rain to plan our course of action.

Winter Park Resort has terrain for all ages and skill levels. From slow easygoing green runs to super steep technical double blacks, there's something for everyone. I could have started out on a green and probably should have, but I didn't want to be bored, and besides I had water-skied before. My naive mind concluded it was mostly the same concept, so for my first ski run ever I chose a long blue run called White Rabbit. I knew the basic ski slang, that to slow down make a pizza slice by bringing the tips of your skis together in a triangle, and to go faster keep them parallel like a french fry. I tried this method and again promptly fell. I would get up, slide at a good pace, speed up, get scared, try to stop, and inevitably fall again. This charade played on repeat for the first 200 yards. My legs and my butt were already sore, and I had barely any progress to show for it. To catch my breath, I sat in the snow on the side of the slope and watched people whiz by, trying to catch how they moved their body to turn into a stop (I later learned this is called Hockey Stopping.) *Alright*, I thought, *you can do this*.

I was going to try and go a little bit farther before falling this time. After standing up, I pointed my skis downhill in the french fry position and picked up quite a bit of speed before realizing I couldn't continue in one direction and didn't know how to turn. My left ski went left while the right stayed straight and I somehow flipped completely around and fell backwards, hard, down the slope and into the trees on the side of the run. This time I lost both skis and had to hike back up the 100 yards I had slid to get them.

This is NOTHING like water skiing..., I thought angrily as I hiked up the hill in my ski boots. *This is stupid.*

Those who saw my wipeout stopped to see if I was okay, and I waved them off with a curt thank-you. One smartass on a snowboard flew by and yelled, "Hey man you should have pizza-ed."

I wished I had a whole pizza to throw at his fathead. After much struggling to get both skis back on, I didn't want to french fry or pizza. My legs felt more like spaghetti, and I just wanted to be back at the bottom. One of the Mountain Hosts must have seen the despair in my stance because she skied up next to me and asked if I needed any help.

"Well... yes, desperately," I answered. "Actually, this is my first time out."

"This season?" the host asked.

"No... ever," I replied shamefully.

Her eyes widened, and my expression fell a little. Clearly, she wasn't expecting to help this much and probably regretted stopping. But she gave me some advice on turning, by gradually rotating both skis into the same direction and concentrating on controlling the pressure to my edges. Edges... that was a new term for me. I thanked her and said it was the only advice I had received, so it had to help.

Well, you could have put roller blades on a baby giraffe and probably would have had the same result.

I tried what the kind Host had said, but ended up crisscrossing the tips of my skis and launching myself forward, head over boots into the snow.

Ouch.

At this point my only goal was to get to the bottom not on a ski patrol sled.

This whole time, Rain had been riding in front and stopped to wait patiently for me after every circus performance. It seemed like forever, but after an hour and forty minutes, I made it to the base of the mountain exhausted, mentally drained and sore from bruises in places I had never had a bruise before. I hobbled over to the edge of the walkway and collapsed in a heap. Rain helped to keep my balance while I unclicked those godforsaken skis, and slowly we made our way back to the car.

I don't know what Trevor had been talking about, this was a nightmare. Hopefully, next time would be more successful, but as far as I was concerned, skiing was the farthest from fun, and I had had enough of it for that entire week.

When I retold my struggle of an adventure to Trevor that night, I could tell he was holding back laughing. Luckily, he didn't give me any crap for it, because my poor broken body would not have taken it well.

"Hey, at least you got out there, though; you didn't panic and give up either," he said, encouraging me.

"Yeah, I won't be going out again unless it's with someone who knows how to ski and can instruct me on what the hell I'm supposed to be doing."

~...~...~

Chapter 5
About Mika

Fortunately, I met such a guy a week later. Rain was having a party that Friday night, Trevor and I were going, along with a few of our friends and coworkers. When we arrived, I was introduced to a handful of guys who all worked the night shift or ran lifts at the resorts. One of them was Mika. He initially stood out to me because he didn't have a scraggly ski-bum beard like the rest of them. His face was clean-shaven and jet-black hair fell around his face in loose curls. He was tall and gangly, leaning against the counter with dark aviator sunglasses on. He had a Pabst beer can in one hand, reaching out to shake mine with the other.

"Hey, I'm Mika," he said with a smile.

"Hi, I'm Natalie, nice to meet you."

He set his beer down and pushed his sunglasses up onto the top of his head, and when I glanced back up, I couldn't help but stare. His eyes were so strikingly blue they caught me off guard. His olive complexion and dark hair made them all the brighter. It wasn't a typical blue either; they were that vivid blue you see in the gaze of some Siberian Huskies or Australian Shepherds, like the color of ice inside a glacier. He gave me a puzzled grin, and realizing I was staring for too long, I stammered out, "Oh... I... um... I'm sorry, it's just... well." I was stumbling over my words. I paused to look down at my thumbs, took a breath and tried again. "I know we literally just met. But holy smokes your eyes are gorgeous."

His grin turned to a laugh, and he turned slightly as his face flushed.

"Wow. Thank you... um," he said bashfully. Now he was the one struggling for words. "I'm sorry, I'm not great at receiving compliments," he continued. "I know I have crazy eyes. Honestly, it's why I wear shades all the time. But most folks just awkwardly stare and don't say anything, so really… thank you."

"Any time." I smiled back

The night carried on with the making of tacos and mixing of margaritas. Most of the guys, Trevor included, gravitated over to the couch where video gaming ensued.

Remember, Trevor and I were still in a bit of a rut with the whole lack of talking and showing affection thing. Nothing had changed. We weren't mad for any particular reason; we just weren't going out of our way to do anything that wasn't completely necessary. Still, it was a little disheartening to see him go over and play games like I wasn't even there. Honestly, he had barely paid me any attention the entire night. Whatever.

I shrugged it off and moved to the bar stool where the stereo was to play DJ. I scrolled through my phone looking for the next song when I felt the floor give slightly, as when someone sits down in the chair very close to you. Mika had chosen not to play video games like the rest, and so we sat at the counter talking about life in Colorado. He told me about moving out on his own and how he had come to the Rockies for the legendary skiing, which inevitably led to me re-playing my dramatic skiing experience from the previous week. When my story was over and we both finished laughing, he informed me that he used to be a ski instructor at his previous job and offered to give me a lesson if I wanted.

"Oh my gosh. That would be soooo great," I said probably a little too enthusiastically. I was on my third margarita and tended to get more animated when I drank.

"Yeah, let me know whenever you'd like to give skiing another go, and I'd be happy to help; maybe save you a few ibuprofens next time, eh?"

"Ha. Ha. For real, though, thank you so much," I exclaimed. "Are you busy next Friday?"

"Works for me," he replied. "Can I get your number so you can let me know time and place?"

"Oh, yeah sure thing!"

I gave Mika my number, and shortly after the gaming party broke apart, either to go home or they had fallen asleep. As Trevor and I walked out the door, I waved to Mika and thanked him again for offering to give me ski lessons.

"No problem," he said. "I look forward to it."

It could have been the tequila, but driving home I felt genuinely excited for the first time in a while. Not only was I going skiing Friday, I was getting a private lesson for free. That night while lying in bed, I listened to Trevor's slow steady breathing, and while he slept, my mind wandered out the window to the clear night sky. But as I drifted off to sleep, the last thing I saw were those piercing blue eyes.

~...~...~

The week flew by, and before I knew it, Friday was here. I woke up ready to conquer the mountain. With nerves at a minimum, I drove to the resort and met Mika down by the employee locker room. Together we slid over to the first lift of the day. He showed me how to use the skis like skates on the flat areas, so it wasn't such a workout to just get to the lift.

"Think of your skis like knives, and you're spreading peanut butter on toast," he had said. It was a good analogy and took me a minute, but I got the hang of it, and started to glide over the snow much quicker and with less effort. He suggested a beginner's green slope, which I willingly agreed to.

At the top, I lost balance trying to get off the lift again but regained control and didn't fall. Already a small victory! This area was much more open and not nearly as steep as where Rain and I were before. The first twenty minutes we worked on form and how to hold the ski poles. It's amazing how much I didn't know. Once we started moving, he told me to think about the direction I wanted to turn and try to move my toes that way while keeping my upper body pointing straight ahead. Since I wasn't moving very fast, it was easier to focus on my direction instead of panicking about speed. To better give instruction, Mika skied backward to watch my progress. Soon enough we had made it to the final downhill pitch of the run.

Wow, I thought, *I'm nearly to the bottom and only fell three times!* Granted I was just creeping along, and my turns were slow, but it was ten times better than my previous ski day.

"So, you want to ride down and try this again?" Mika asked.

He had been so patient and encouraging this whole time. I thought he must have been a great coach. "Yes. Definitely," I replied

We repeated that slope three more times with Mika backwards skiing down in front and giving pointers. Each time I got a little faster and was becoming familiar with using the edge of the skis for control. By the end of the day my confidence elevated and my outlook on Alpine Skiing had changed for the better. I still was only comfortable on greens, and knew I had a long way to go, but with any sport it's progress not perfection. I noticed too that Mika seemed just as pleased with my performances as I was. Back at the base of the resort, before going our separate ways, he gave me a tight hug.

Mm, he smells good, I mentally noted.

He praised me again on my efforts for the day, and with a wave said he couldn't wait for our next session. I waved back, then tromping up to the parking lot realized I hadn't said when the next time would be. But I guess that's a good thing, I had thoroughly enjoyed my lesson and apparently didn't even have to ask for another.

~...~...~

When I told Trevor about my success that day, he, too, was thrilled and said he was glad Mika could show me how to ski because he himself wasn't a great teacher. I knew this but chose not to comment. Trevor had a tendency to be a bit jealous, and I was worried he would be uncomfortable with another guy taking me out to ski. But luckily Trevor and Mika got along great! They had gone out skiing multiple times and became fast friends. During Trevor's lunch breaks, they would come visit me at work. (I could stealthily get them free food.)

We both found good company in Mika, and tension between Trevor and I stared to loosen. He was happy because he had found a skiing buddy equal to his level, and I had someone to coach me, as well as talk to. (You may not know it, but riding up ski lifts is a great time to get to know someone. Especially if the lift stops and your sitting suspended twenty-five feet in the air for ten minutes.) I should have realized that I was talking more and more with Mika and less with Trevor, but because someone was listening and held interest in what I had to say again, I, too, was happier. The little pet peeves I held against Trevor didn't bother me anymore.

My conversations with Mika started off just being about my lessons, but gradually turned to other interests, casual remarks about our day, and the occasional innocent flirting. Witty comments, low-key compliments, a winky face instead of a smiley face all became more frequent in our text messages. I knew by now he had a thing for me, and if I'm being honest, I had a small crush on him too.

But it's not like this will turn into anything, I told myself. With he and Trevor being so close now, I thought once my lessons stopped, Mika would start thinking of me as just a friend. Not to mention his buddy's girlfriend. But the frequent texting didn't stop. I had no intention of leaving Trevor, yet I continued to shamelessly flirt with Mika. It was one of those "too good to be true" situations and eventually, within a short amount of time, came to a crashing halt.

~…~…~

Trevor and I were standing in the kitchen making breakfast when he got a text from Mika. Moments later my phone beeped, and I glanced down to read:

"Hi. So, got an awesome new job, no more cleaning floors at Winter Park! I'll be leaving Colorado in 2 weeks." Instantly my face fell, and I got that feeling you get when you find out your vacation's been cut short or when that show on Netflix you've been looking forward to for weeks gets canceled. I looked up to see Trevor was also sad; he was losing a good friend but had no idea I was losing something more. For his last week in town, Mika wanted to take a weekend trip out to Steamboat for one final day on the mountain. So, a group of guys, along with Trevor, drove out on a Saturday afternoon. I left after work with Rain to meet them the following night.

Steamboat Resort didn't have as many beginners runs as Winter Park, so I was on the struggle bus for most of the day. I was very frustrated with myself and got particularly upset with Trevor because he said to follow them down a black diamond tree run. I was not prepared. All the nerves and fear returned as I half rolled, half side stepped all the way down. I felt terrible for holding up the guys who were much better than I was. But they all seemed pretty cool about it. Mika assured me they had gotten in a hard day's riding yesterday, so they didn't mind waiting.

Regardless, it was still a long day, and by the end everyone was ready to relax in the room and have a few drinks. Trevor was sitting right next to me on the bed and because of the whiskey I was not being so discreet with my texting. Trevor could see every message Mika and I were sending each other across the room. I don't know if he could make out exactly what each said but can guarantee that it wasn't a "just friends" conversation.

Eventually we all passed out and woke up the next morning to a loud knocking on the hotel room door. In his drunkenness, one of the guys had left the room in the middle of the night to make a phone call, but locked himself out and instead of knocking, went to the front desk and just bought another room for himself. He had no recollection of this, but the lady behind the computer in the lobby later confirmed his purchase.

While Trevor was in the shower I looked back through my texts to Mika and quickly deleted them, hoping that Trevor hadn't seen. But in my gut, there was a sinking feeling telling me that he had.... But I wasn't going to talk about this now with everyone around. So, I put it out of my mind for the time being.

The carpool drive back was uneventful, but I could tell Trevor's laughs and smiles were forced.

Shit, he knows, I thought.

It was late when we got home, and he didn't mention anything about me and Mika. We both were wiped, so nothing was said. The following day I woke up and Trevor had already left for work.

That morning Mika texted and said he wanted to see me once more before he left. I didn't have to be at the café until later that day, so shortly before my shift started, I went over to see him, thinking I would make this a quick goodbye. Naturally, he was home alone.

I walked inside, and we sat on his couch in an awkward silence for a few moments. I didn't know what to expect coming over here.

"I'm going to miss you," he said, twirling his hair with two fingers and breaking the silence.

"I'll miss you too.... I'm glad we met, though, I mean, without your expertise I would still be a hazard to everyone on the mountain," I said, trying to lighten the mood.

He paused again, then let out a loud sigh.

"I wish things were different," he breathed softly.

I didn't respond right away, and he looked up, with more intensity this time.

"I really like you, Natalie. You know you're not like other girls." Another pause, then he continued. "I mean do you even want to be with Trevor?"

His question really hit me. I felt an unexpected wave of annoyance, partly towards Mika, partly towards myself.

"Yes," I said curtly. "Yes, I do. I don't want to break up with him. I'm sorry, Mika," I said, not meeting his gaze. I had strung him along like a puppy. The game was fun, but now I was ending it, metaphorically slamming the door in his face. My stomach started to hurt.

He looked very glum, and I wanted to leave. For a painful minute we stayed at this standstill before I said I should go.

I stood up to walk to the door, and he followed. Standing in the open doorway. I turned to say goodbye, and in one fluid motion he grabbed my hand, pulled me back so that we were face-to-face, wrapped his arms around my waist, and kissed me, for a long moment I kissed him back.

Oh my God Oh my God Oh my God.

All kinds of mental alarms started going off inside my head. I pulled away, stepped outside and half jogged, half tripped up to the car.

Fuck, that was NOT how that was supposed to go, I thought as I pulled out onto the road.

That entire day was all a blur. Why did I let this happen? It was like getting slapped in the face and dowsed with ice water all at once. I couldn't decide if I wanted to cry or throw up. All I could think about was Mika kissing me. That night on the way home neither Trevor nor I spoke until we pulled up to the house. He was still sulking from the Steamboat trip, and I was super nervous about the conversation to come. He turned the car off but didn't get out.

"What's bothering you, babe?" I asked, hoping he would bring up the obvious.

"Nothing, I just have a lot on my mind."

"Trevor come on. I can tell somethings wrong"

"Okay… yeah there is something wrong." I waited, but he said nothing further.

"This is about Mika."

"Yes!" he retorted loudly. "What's been going on between you guys?" he asked. That sinking-stomach feeling came back again.

"God… I'm sorry, Trevor. I didn't think it would come to this…." And then it all came out. I told him how it started with the ski lessons and how I liked the attention and having someone to talk to. I told him about the flirting, and how I could have stopped it but didn't want to. Finally, I told him about that morning and the kiss. Once I was done rambling, I thought I would feel better, but the look on Trevor's face nearly pushed me to tears. He was disappointed, and he was hurt.

True, he had become distant and less affectionate over the past few months, but I was just as much to blame for not trying to communicate. He had never done anything seriously wrong and would never think of looking at another girl. Meanwhile I had taken advantage of his trust and used it to my advantage for my own selfishness. The weight of my mistake was weighing down very heavily. He processed that truth for what felt like a long while, and then said something I was not prepared for.

"I'm sorry too. If I had been better to you, none of this would have happened."

Wait. What?! Is he serious? This man is blaming himself.

"Whoa, stop," I said. "Don't try to say for a second that this is your fault. Sure, I guess you're partially right, but I am waaaay more to blame than you are. You should be mad at me!" When I said this, I pointed very aggressively towards myself and accidently jabbed a finger in my eye.

Now a hint of a smile showed on his lips.

"I'm not mad at you," he said, staring at the steering wheel, trying hard to hold back a laugh. "But I'm sorry I didn't say anything sooner. I don't want this to happen again."

"It won't, I promise. Cross my heart," I said with watery eyes. (really it was just my left eye; the right was spared self-assault.) He smiled for real this time.

The snow continued to fall outside making a soft pitter-patter of flakes on the windshield. I reached across the center console and grabbed his hand.

"I love you, ya know," I said, looking down at our interlocked fingers, running the side of my thumb along the top of his.

"I love you too." He sighed. "I'm just glad Mika is gone, because I would have a really hard time seeing him now." He looked over at me. "Want to go inside?"

"Yes." I smiled back.

Following Trevor into our basement apartment that night, I made a mental note to not take my boyfriend for granted. It's easy to forget the good in tough situations, but Trevor brought so much good to our relationship. I was so very lucky to have a guy like him, who loved me unconditionally, trusted me without question, made me laugh until I cried, and never thought twice about loving another girl. I had forgotten that so quickly when a new temptation arose, but for now I had learned my lesson.

~...~...~

Chapter 6
About Getting Kicked Out

That winter passed by very quickly. With every new rush of tourists and vacationers, work stayed busy for us. Getting to go out about once a week with Trevor and Rain, I got progressively better on skis, and the three of us all got to be very close friends. One afternoon at the end of March, we were all headed to the basement apartment for a quick bite before hitting the slopes again. I walked into the laundry room to check on my clothes in the dryer, and there lying on the counter was a two-page typed letter from our landlords. In that letter was a request no tenant ever wants to hear, but before I continue, let me explain a few prior events that led up to this moment. Are you ready? Here goes.

When Trevor and I first moved in, as you know there was a sunroom, and inside said sunroom were two plants that Peggy had been growing for a while. I asked if we would be responsible for taking care of these plants during our six-month stay. Trevor had been working in landscaping since before high school, so remembering to water a tree and a bush every now and then shouldn't have been a problem. Happily, we had agreed.

Keep in mind, though, it said nothing in the lease about tending to the landlord's plants. We had no trouble with them for the first couple of months (granted Trevor did most of the work, and I admittingly forgot to water them a few times). All was well until one night, after we had been out skiing the whole day and decided to split a joint before unwinding. We didn't smoke very often at this apartment; it was usually just with friends or the occasional edible. (It took me a few times to decide if I even liked weed or not, turned out I was going about it all wrong, but we'll get to that later.) When we did partake, we would go out to the sunroom, close the door connecting it to the basement, open a window and blow the smoke outside. This particular night was no different except that when we left, we didn't close the window all the way, letting the freezing cold air seep into the room.

The next day I had an email from Peggy saying that she had been in the yard that morning and noticed the window was ajar. She asked that we make sure to keep it closed. No big deal. Peggy then went on to remind us that smoking cigarettes was NOT permitted on the property. Apparently, Vernon had found cigarette butts in the driveway and assumed that it was from us. Trevor and I have never smoked cigarettes; however, we had had a friend over a couple nights previous who did. I replied to Peggy informing her of this, apologized for our friend's carelessness in littering and assured her neither of us would break the lease on that matter.

A week later I walked into the sunroom and noticed the green on the leaves of the trees were starting to turn yellow and the branches had more of a droop than before.

Oh no..., I thought. *I've killed their tree.*

Frantically I got the watering can, filled it up and poured it slowly over the tree's roots. The soil was very dry, so the water soaked in almost instantly.

Don't panic; it still has a chance.

Later, Trevor looked at it, and he said it could still be saved. We just needed to water it and try to get more sun to it. Well, the poor tree didn't have a chance. My thumb was about as green as a stop sign. My lack of watering didn't help the fact that it was not an indoor tree to begin with, and without freezing temperatures, sunlight in a Colorado winter can be hard to come by. Two weeks later, the tree was dead. No question, flatlined, done sauce.

As if on cue, I received another email from Peggy. Why she never spoke to us in person was beyond me. After the cigarette incident, Peggy and Vernon ceased personal interaction. She was very blatant in saying how devastated she was with the loss of this tree. According to her, it had been in the sun room for five years without issue. Then Trevor and I come along with the secret intention of killing it in cold blood. She blamed it on the night that we left the window opened and let in the cold, going on and on, making it sound as if we had run over their dog.

I wasn't sure what Peggy wanted me to do. I waited to reply until after I'd read the email to Trevor. We agreed that if our landlords wanted, we would remove the dead tree and replace it with a new one of their choice. Thinking this would appease them, I sent my apologies along with our proposal to give them a new tree. Well, they didn't want a new plant, they just wanted us to dispose of the dead one. For them it just couldn't be replaced, the pain was too deep.

You think I'm exaggerating, don't you? Believe me I wish I were.

I was disappointed we had upset our landlords, but it was hard to feel guilty. Yes, I neglected to water it, which was probably the true cause of death, not leaving the window open that one night. Besides, if the stupid thing meant so much to them, why leave it in the hands of two tenants you barely know? Regardless of the reasons, trust was gone, and feelings were hurt. This was strike two.

After that they stopped communication all together. Even waiting to leave the house until Trevor and I were gone. The also asked that we leave rent money on the laundry room counter instead of handing it to them in person.

~ ... ~ ... ~

The laundry room became our portal of communication. It was here that we received strike three. Earlier that week, while putting a beer delivery away in the bar storage dry room, Rain mentioned what a hassle it was not having a washer and dryer in his apartment. I told him that Trevor was at home, and after he got off work, he was welcome to wash a load of clothes there. He had never asked before and I didn't see the harm in letting a good friend wash one load of laundry. Again, I was wrong. When he came over, I was still at the resort, but Trevor was there at the apartment. Waiting for his clothes to finish their cycle, Rain hung out in the living room, but when he went to switch things from the washer to the dryer, Peggy chose that moment to come get more towels for the upstairs bathroom. She opened the door to find Rain, a stranger, in her laundry room. According to him she seemed shocked and when he told her he was a friend of ours, was only doing one load and then leaving, she became very reserved. She told Rain that this was highly inappropriate and then left. He told Trevor, but neither he nor I heard anything about it that day or the next. Assuming there was no problem, we thought little of the incident.

The reason we had heard nothing from our landlords was because they were taking the time to write the letter we found on the counter that afternoon. Not only was Peggy upset about Rain using their washing machine, she was, I quote: "Appalled at the disrespect for their property and safety." According to her, Rain was a potentially dangerous man who obviously just waltzed into their home because we didn't lock the door. They didn't even think to ask if Trevor and I had invited him in, or if we were home at the time he came over. Rain also had an electronic vape mod in his pocket, which Peggy referred to as a marijuana smoking device. True, the lease said no smoking, but last time I checked that doesn't mean we couldn't have a friend over with cigarettes or a vape mod in a pocket. Not once did Rain use it on their property. Peggy went on to say that we could not be trusted. Again, I quote: "Young Trevor is too immature to follow simple requests."

Wow, I thought. *These people are more uptight than I realized.*

Just for good measure they brought up the tree again. Probably to reaffirm our immaturity in writing.

My God! Can't they let it go?!

Peggy ended the letter by saying that they wished us the best in our future endeavors, but suggested we find a new place to stay by the end of the month.

Damn, I thought. *Well, I guess we're not getting our security deposit back.*

Time to start apartment hunting again.

It wasn't worth our effort to try and change our landlord's minds. They were dead set on us leaving. I started searching for a new place right away. Fortunately finding an apartment was much easier when we already were living in the area. This time of the year, it seemed everyone was leaving Winter Park for their summer jobs. Lucky for Trevor and I, this meant lots of options. We skimmed through a few adds and found one that was in Fraser, a town only six miles down Highway 40 from Winter Park. It was closer to Safeway and the Shell gas station. Plus, all utilities were included in the rent. The only hiccup was that it was a three bedroom and we only needed one, but every other place we looked at was either too expensive, didn't include heat or electric, or was simply run down. We knew we didn't have the time to be picky, but we also didn't want to go broke or live in a dump. So, we came to the conclusion to look at the three bedrooms, and if we liked it, would ask Rain if he wanted to be our roommate.

His lease was coming to a close, so he too was looking for new living accommodations. This way the three of us could afford rent, and the sooner we signed a new lease the sooner we could leave Peggy and Vernon. Rain was all aboard, so the next afternoon Trevor and I went to meet with Richard and Julie, the owners of the apartment. Not only was this couple night-and-day different from our previous landlords, but they didn't live on the floor directly above us.

What was once a large house had been turned into a four-unit apartment complex. It was in a nice neighborhood, had plenty of parking space and a decent sized backyard complete with a firepit. They both were kind and welcoming and answered all our questions. The only requirements Richard and Julie had were no pets, no criminals, pay your rent on time, and don't burn down the building. That day Trevor, Rain, and I signed a new lease.

I was so relieved to have found a suitable apartment so quickly. The next step was to speed pack and move out as soon as possible. For the short amount of time we were given from Vernon and Peggy, Trevor and I thought we did a damn good job of cleaning the basement. It looked exactly as it did before we arrived (minus the tree) I even shampooed parts of the carpet and scrubbed the floor of the kitchen with a toothbrush. It was immaculate, but Vernon and Peggy still said in a later email they had to have their basement professionally cleaned because we were such animals. Vernon said he had to check to see if his cat was okay after seeing the inside of the microwave. Which was total bullshit. (I mean seriously, how petty can you get?) For heaven's sake we were gone! I never did like Snowball, or Fluffy, or whatever his name was, (if the door leading upstairs was left open a crack, he liked to slink in and hide in the small space between the cabinet top and kitchen ceiling. He then would wait until an unsuspecting tenant was washing dishes or opening the refrigerator to superman-jump onto the floor mere inches from their feet. He once narrowly missed a bottle of Chardonnay to the head, only because I decided he wasn't worth the loss of wine.) but I wasn't sadistic enough to microwave him as a parting gift.

All that ridiculousness aside, we were done with them and happily settling into a new apartment with more space and no landlords constantly hovering.

~...~...~

Chapter 7
About the Couch

The new place in Fraser was a bit of a mess the first week. Since we had to move so fast, clothes and personal items were just dumped into rooms. Wine and beer boxes I'd snagged from work and filled with cups, dishes, towels, and other household appliances lined the walls of our new kitchen. Days off were spent organizing and unpacking until eventually we had it looking more like a home instead of a thrift store warehouse. Besides a lonely computer desk, the apartment was unfurnished. So, Trevor and I found ourselves driving down to Denver to go furniture shopping at IKEA. We didn't go to the city very often, but when we had an excuse to, we made a day of it. It ended up being a fun afternoon and successful trip. We had found everything we were looking for and didn't go over our budget. The rest of the furniture that wouldn't fit in the Escape, such as bed frames, dressers and an entertainment center, we got from friends or Facebook Swap. The only piece we didn't have was a couch. We wanted a sectional to go in the back bedroom that had been turned into a living area/game room. At the time we were just sitting on a spare mattress to watch movies. I did some Googling, took a lot of measurements, made a few phone calls and decided to order a couch online. It was a bit risky cause it's not like I could send it back if it didn't fit, but if all went well, I would be saving a lot of money, and it would be delivered to our door instead of having to figure out a way to transport it ourselves.

It was a two-piece sectional, and on the scheduled day of delivery, I was waiting at the door when the truck arrived. The driver was very professional, he double-checked all the information with me, but when he went around and opened the doors on the back of the truck there was only one piece of the furniture inside.

"Um… where is the other half of the couch?" I asked. "This was supposed to be a two-piece sectional."

The driver became frazzled.

"Oh, um, well I'm not sure, ma'am," he stuttered, "this was all that was on the order to be loaded. I can move this piece inside for you and then give you the direct number to call and find out. But I'm just the delivery man."

"Fine, that's fine," I said. "Thank You." There was no sense berating the poor driver. I knew he wouldn't have the answers. The half that did show up was indeed what I had ordered; it just would look a lot better if I had the other.

I spent the next three hours on the phone only to find out the furniture company I ordered from went out of business. There was no way I was getting the other half of my couch; however, they did give me a complete refund. So, I got my money back, but now we were left with one section of a two-piece sectional couch. It could be worse, I guess. At least the half we got was the longer of the two, I could make it work; I was sure of it.

The logical next course of action would be to wait for Rain and Trevor to get home from work so we could move it to the back room. Of course, me being the woman that I was, thought I could move it from the entryway, through the kitchen, to the very back of the apartment by myself.

To fully appreciate the following story, you readers should know that the couch was longer than the short narrow hallway it needed to fit through. I tried turning it sideways, upside down, sliding it on its back, nothing worked. It was simply too wide. The doors would need to come off, so I went to get a screwdriver, but realized that Trevor had his toolbox with him at work in the Escape. At this point I really should have stopped and waited for him to get home. Some might say stubborn, but I say I was determined. This had turned into a mission, and I was bound to finish it.

So, I set to work removing the door with a pocketknife and a garlic press. (This is all fact I promise.) By unscrewing the screws slightly with the knife, I could loosen it enough to grab it with the garlic press and turn it the rest of the way like a makeshift wrench. Not exactly practical, but resourceful. After much turning and pulling and shimmying I got the door off and set it in our bedroom. (It was more of a "drop" than a "set" though; the slab was more solid than it looked.)

This gave me barely enough space to squeeze the couch through and around the corner to the last hallway leading to the game room. Getting it down this particular stretch was painless, but the door to the backroom was set at an angle. I hadn't noticed the odd architecture of this house until I was trying to maneuver a heavy, awkward piece of furniture through it. But I had gotten past one door already, why would this one be any different? I swear the thing had a brain and heard what I was thinking, because it would NOT go through that final door. Again, I turned it every which way, climbed over the back cushions multiple times to pull and twist until I had run out of curse words, was sweating and even bleeding from scrapes on my knees and elbows. I was clean out of energy and motivation. I thought briefly of chopping it into firewood with the axe outside. Knowing I wasn't getting any farther, I decided to leave it to the boys to figure out.

So, after texting Trevor about the dilemma I was now passing on to him, I climbed back over the couch and turned to observe my handiwork. I had left it at an angle where the back of the couch was facing the ceiling with about two feet of clearance. The only way to get to the game room door was by crawling through the tunnel formed by the headrest leaning against the wall and the arm of the couch resting against the floor. It was comical really. I left to go for a run and looked forward to my boyfriend's response.

I ran until my frustration had subsided, and feeling tired but no longer murderous, I walked back into the apartment to find Rain and Trevor casually lounging on the couch in the game room as if it had been there all along. Dumbfounded I started, mouth gaping at them in disbelief

"How. In the hell. Did you get that monstrosity in here?" I questioned

Trevor didn't take his eyes off the TV when he answered. "Well you left it wedged in the hall pretty tight, but I just turned it a little bit and pushed it through the doorway."

"That's not possible," I said, still in utter denial. "I went to battle with that couch trying to get it in here."

"Sometimes it just takes a different approach, my dear," he said with a smirk.

Convinced it was magic, I inspected the wall and doorframe to see no signs of a struggle. How he did it, I will never know; some things are just left a mystery.

~...~...~

Chapter 8
About Brandon and Molly

In our new neighborhood, there were many people close to our own age. Unlike our previous neighbors, there were no complaints about late nights and loud music. One such neighbor was Brandon, who lived in the house immediately to the right of us. We would frequently go over to his home after a long day of riding for drinks and a joint, or to work on ski/snowboard gear. Sometimes Rain would sing and play his guitar while the rest of us made food for a cookout.

Brandon can only be described as a rambling vagabond man. He was a year older than Trevor and I and six foot five with a mop of shaggy brown hair that always was a touch out of place. He loved anything that involved a motor and had absolutely zero fear when it came to extreme sports. He was raised in Tennessee but drifted to Colorado where he grew very skilled in his already great rafting and kayaking abilities. It wasn't uncommon to hear a dirt bike screaming down the roads behind our apartment and know it was Brandon, out for a cruise at breakneck speed. He had a laid-back personality, but no patience for drama. The best thing about meeting Brandon though, was getting to also meet his four-legged companion, Jack. This little dude was a playful, super friendly, adorable corgi/jack Russell terrier mix. The pup had the coloring of a Jack Russell, including a heart on his butt, with the fluffy body and curled tail of a corgi. He was overly enthusiastic at the introduction of a new human, and I instantly fell in love with him. The four of us (Brandon, Trevor, Jack, and I) made many memories that summer, some stemming from not great decisions. Which leads to the next chapter of this story.

~...~...~

Growing up in a small town, with schooling based in traditional Catholic values, I never gave a single thought to try drugs. It was just something you didn't do. In my upbringing, those who had indulged we're called lowlifes, crackheads, white trash, the list of slurs goes on.

Nothing about drugs other than the caffeine in coffee appealed to me until I came to Colorado, where not only marijuana, but other substances were easy to come by. Some of those being not-so-legal. One afternoon Rain walked into the kitchen from his room and casually asked if Trevor and I had ever tried Molly before. Neither of us had, and we shook our heads wondering where he was going with his question.

"Well, I got some from a buddy of mine and was hoping the three of us could go skiing, and maybe have a little extra fun while we're at it," he said with a grin.

Wow didn't see that coming today.

Trevor and I exchanged glances, shrugged and answered with, "Uh, sure why not!" I couldn't believe I was agreeing to this, but I trusted Rain wholeheartedly and knew he wouldn't try to convince me to do something that would harm me or Trevor.

Rain unfortunately had a pretty colored past. He didn't have much guidance or stability as a child and therefore grew up fast, having to learn difficult truths about the world on his own. He was fiercely independent, but in his teens got into a lot of trouble, some of it with the law. He's since then turned over a new leaf but had many experiences with Molly and other drugs in his adolescence. He assured us the dosage we would be taking was so small it would only last a few hours at the most.

In case you are wondering, Molly is slang for Molecular, and refers to MDMA or Ecstasy. Once ingested it increases the brains production of dopamine, norepinephrine, and serotonin, which are chemicals your body naturally produces when you're excited, happy, or looking at something/someone you love. Basically, it releases a lot of happy feelings all at once. Thus, giving the taker a euphoric sensation of blissful invincibility. Perfect for skiing, right?

The following day we all were off work, so we loaded up and headed to the resort. In the parking lot, we each took one dose. Rain took a little more than Trevor I because his body already had a tolerance. It was in crystal salt form and tasted terrible, exceptionally bitter, like chewing a pill that's meant to be swallowed, but after an orange juice chaser we were ready to ride.

Typically, Molly will take thirty to forty minutes before it kicks in, and it did so for me before the guys. Riding up the lift, I remembered looking at the snow-covered treetops, tall pines swaying in the slight breeze, and there, nestled in the fluff was a blackbird. It held a pinecone in its beak, and to my newly influenced mind that was hilarious. I started laughing at the bird and was suddenly very amped to get my feet on the snow and start riding. Even with heavy boots and skis dangling off the edge of the chair, my legs felt weightless. The lift just couldn't move fast enough. As soon as we were off and onto the slope the guys suggested High Lonesome trees to ride first, which to me, was still a fairly nerve-wracking area. I wasn't comfortable yet skiing through trees, but now I thought it was the perfect idea. Energy was surging through my body like I had just taken shots of espresso spiked with adrenaline. I couldn't stand still any longer. I sailed through the entrance of the tree run, weaving in and out and around the pines and cedars as if I had been doing this all season. Not a hint of anxiety entered my mind as I flew towards the first opening. When I exploded out of the trees, I caught some air, spun around, landed backwards and slid into a hockey stop next to Rain and Trevor.
!!!!!!!!!!!!!

"Ohmygod!" I shouted in one word. "That. Was. Exhilarating."

It really was. I smiled so big for so long that my cheeks started to hurt, but I didn't care. I wanted to ski, I wanted to fly, I wanted to gain enough speed to make my eyes stream tears behind my goggles. With a jump and a twist, we were back in the trees, the guys feeling pretty sensational themselves by now. It was during this afternoon while rolling on Molly that I truly felt the joy of skiing for the first time. All the obstacles that caused hesitation in me before, were now an inviting new challenge. Fear felt foreign, nonexistent, like the sensation one gets right after kissing someone they love for the first time or when you're in a neck-and-neck track race and pull forward to win at the last second. Imagine that feeling lasting for two hours, so many good emotions the thought of frustration was laughable.

And oh, how we laughed. Bolting out of the trees and down the smooth groomed run to the bottom, I whooped and hollered, cloaked in pure bliss. I shouted to Trevor and Rain that I loved them both, and they shouted back that they loved me too. It was a silly afternoon amidst a perfect day. By the time we left we were back to a normal state of mind, and the three of us felt a little closer. I had overcome some of my qualms about skiing, and we all were very optimistic about the coming week. I never would have guessed a drug would result in such a bonding experience.

Having shared this story I feel obligated to say that I don't in any way condone taking Molly to overcome your fears. I didn't know what to expect, but I was in a positive frame of mind to begin with. Therefore, the sensational serotonin boosts only heightened what I was already feeling. I haven't taken Molly since that afternoon, it was a memorable day, but not one I've repeated.

~…~…~

Chapter 9
About Parents

That month held a lot of firsts for me. From learning to love skiing, gaining more experience work, (I was now running the entire kitchen) to having a long-distance relationship with my parents. Which is what I want to talk about next.

It was strange at first, but soon a call once or twice a week back home became the norm. Every time I would ask when they would come to see us. Eventually I got the text from my mom saying they would be visiting our mountain town that April. *Finally!* I was starting to think my parents wouldn't make it out that year, but now I was very much looking forward to that week.

The night they arrived, I gave Jonathan his belated birthday present, led them on a grand tour of our semi-clean apartment and then just took some time to catch up and share stories. My family was pretty tired from the drive, so they turned in early. The next day Trevor and I showed them around Winter Park and took them to the resort to see the mountain. My mom, Jonathan, and I did a little bit of skiing (mostly because they didn't want to go back to Illinois and say they hadn't tried) but after an hour on the slopes, they were ready to rest until dinner. We went to Randy's Restaurant that evening, a great American-Irish-style place with decent prices that my dad wouldn't be opposed to. Trevor and I met my family there, and on the way, we discussed how we'd present to them our plans for the coming summer.

Trevor and I wanted to go on a northern vacation that year, possibly Montana or even Alaska and hopefully take Jonathan with us, give him a mountain camping trip he wouldn't forget. We had the basics sorted out and were going to propose the idea to my parents that night. I was channeling good vibes hoping the conversation would go smoothly. Once we ordered and were waiting for our food, I brought up the summer and dove into our idea. I thought I delivered well, and when I finished talking, I expected them to be reasonably impressed or at least not concerned, but instead their faces held no expression.

All right, I thought. *Say something please.*

When they did respond, it was nothing I had anticipated. Apparently, they too, were planning on having a talk with Trevor and I, only theirs was not so uplifting. My dad proceeded to tell us that they were still not supportive or comfortable with Trevor and I living together.

He told me, "You were raised better than this, Natalie. You should know better than to keep living in sin." Since I was no longer living with them, my parents couldn't just punish me, or make me do what they wanted "because it's their house and they said so," but they made clear the extent of their disapproval of my recent life choices. I didn't know what to say.

"Well, what do you want me to do, then," I responded, concentrating hard on my tone of voice. "Because we aren't having any problems living together, and it is not like we are going to move to separate places just because you think it's wrong. Plus, it would be very impractical."

"Well, if you're going to continue to share the same bedroom, then you should be married," my dad responded. He continued with, "If you are not ready for marriage, then you are not ready to share an apartment."

Okay. Hold the phone. Now they were saying that their solution is for us to get married. Then magically everything would be fine. It took all I had not to roll my eyes.

Obviously, their real concern wasn't the act of living in the same apartment; it was having sex outside of wedlock. They just were not going to say that in front of my kid brother. It's true I used to believe that I would wait and stay chaste until marriage. It was easy to say, "Sure I'll 'save myself' for my future spouse" when there wasn't anyone I felt sexually attracted to. It was of no concern to me until I was in my first serious relationship. Needless to say, when I met Trevor, I had a new stance on abstinence before marriage; it still was something I took seriously, but I no longer thought I was going to Hell if I had sex with someone I wasn't bound to via a marriage contract. Fortunately, Trevor felt the same way. I'm not going to go *50 Shades of Grey* on you guys; the sexual aspect of our relationship was fine, more than fine actually, but it wasn't a major priority. To be honest I've never understood what the big deal is. Maybe I'm just the odd girl out, but the act of "doing it" doesn't appeal to me as it seems to appeal to a vast portion of society. Don't get me wrong, when it happened, the sex was great, just not something we (mostly I) saw as a necessity. It's kind of like how vanilla ice cream is delicious on its own, but it's better when you sprinkle some chocolate candy (preferably mini M&M's) on top.

I tried to gently explain this outlook to my parents before, but talking about your sex life with your Mom and Dad is awkward regardless of the situation. But apparently if we were married, they would feel better about it.

Keep in mind my dad said this in front of Trevor, like he was expecting him to get down on one knee right there.

We were at a stalemate. Finally, the food came out, but no one was hungry anymore. I took a moment to collect my thoughts before speaking calmly, "I'm sorry you feel that way, but Trevor and I are very happy together. I hoped you'd be glad I'm in a healthy relationship and financially stable instead of criticizing me for the same thing you have criticized me for before we even moved in together."

My dad looked like he was going to pop a blood vessel, and my mom looked like she was going to cry, but I carried on.

"Trevor and I are not getting married, at least not right now; that would be foolish, and we won't be living apart either. You can't be angry with me for not thinking exactly like you anymore. I'm my own person, and I will form my beliefs based on my own life decisions not yours." When I finished my hands were shaking, and I asked the waiter for a box, we were taking our dinner to go.

I don't know if any of you reading this have had a moment like this with your parents, but if you have, you'll know how diminishing it can make you feel. Like you were presenting them with a homemade gift, and they immediately threw it in the garbage. Driving home that night, I felt defeated. Trevor didn't know what to say, so he silently reached over and squeezed my hand. It was a small gesture, but it made the angry tension coursing through my body subside a little. Maybe a good night's sleep would do everyone some good. We still had one more day before my parents headed home. Lord knows what that was going to be like.

It turned out to be a non-eventful afternoon without any outbursts, or heated arguments like I had envisioned. I mentally brushed the feelings I had from the night before under the rug. Of course, I was still mad, but the intense burning was more of a dull ache now. Besides, I wanted to enjoy the brief time I had with my family before they left.

I took my mom out to do some sightseeing in the surrounding towns, and we met back up with my Dad and Jonathan for lunch. Trevor and I had to work that evening, but I promised to stop by The Trailhead Inn where they were staying after our shifts ended.

That night in my family's hotel room, when Trevor and I said our last goodbyes, the atmosphere was light and optimistic. We talked about skiing and their drive ahead, and I wished them a safe journey home. I knew they were hoping I was no longer upset about the dinner conversation, but those wounds were still fresh. I knew how they felt, there was no doubt there, but I wasn't going back to Illinois until my feelings were expressed in equal proportions.

~...~...~

The next day I sat down with a cup of coffee in our quiet apartment to write a letter to my parents. I've always been better at expressing my true feelings through written words instead of face-to-face. In the letter I told them how much it hurt to hear them say they were disappointed in my life, and not once did they mention they were proud of me for having a good job, a decent place to live, or being in a healthy relationship. I expressed that I knew their concerns with Trevor and I living together, and that it's possible to accept my opinions without ridiculing me for having opinions different from theirs. I wanted very much for my parents to be a part of my life, but if they continued to lecture me on the same issue every time they visited, my trips home would become less and less frequent. Time ticked by, and eventually my hand was cramping from so much writing, erasing, and rewriting, but I had my letter exactly how I wanted it. That afternoon as I dropped it into the out of town slot at the post office, I thought, *well there's no taking that back, only time will tell if this was a good idea.*

~...~...~

Chapter 10
About Tripping... (aka LSD)

In the years prior to moving to Colorado, if you would have asked me if I had ever tripped before, I would have replied with something like "Well, yea... my left shoe comes untied a lot and sometimes when I'm walking, I forget to lift my feet all the way. I fell up (yes, up) the stairs doing this once."

This was before I tried LSD.

You're probably thinking, whoa, wait a minute, you were just talking about your parents, and now were in a chapter on LSD. Yep, that's right kids, I'm talking about drugs again. We're going in chronological order, and this particular part of my timeline was a bit all over the place. So anyway, here in the following pages you'll find the story of my introduction to hallucinogens. It was totally bonkers, and it goes like this.

Once the winter season was over, there was a period in between jobs where we had a good chunk of time off. Many mountain towns refer to this as mud season. We had all been working our asses off for the past six months and needed a break. Brandon, being the avid kayaker he was, knew of a place called Radium Hot Springs. He told us all about the great camping spots, the wildly beautiful scenery, and how the hot spring was nestled in a cove right next to the Colorado River. It sounded wonderful. He also mentioned it was his favorite spot to go tripping. This of course led to a conversation about LSD, and whether or not Trevor, Rain, and I would be game to try some. This would be another first for us, but our experience with Rain had been without harm, so why not take it up a level?

We made plans for a camping trip the following weekend. Rain coincidentally knew someone who could provide him with six tabs of acid. Both

Brandon and Rain had tripped multiple times before, so we trusted our friends to not give us anything we would later regret. Fast forward to that Saturday. The five of us (Jack the dog included) along with two coworkers from Winter Park, drove out to Radium Hot Springs. When we hiked out to our campsite, there was already a couple set up with their tent, but with so much open space we had no problem making camp a little lower down the Valley. (Remember this couple, they will come into play later.)

As promised, Rain pulled six small white tabs wrapped in foil from a zip lock bag in his backpack. We each placed one on our tongue and then waited for things to get weird. It didn't take long. Right away our crew went down to the Hot Springs where we were joined by a boisterous group of river rafters. They drunkenly spilled into the Hot Springs with us and soon everyone was laughing and telling stories like we were all old friends. But then, another raft floated by and pulled up to the bank. The Hot Spring wasn't exactly a large pool, and if these newcomers tried to join, personal space bubbles would start to pop. The woman getting out of the raft wasn't what I would call tiny either. To make matters more interesting, she was traveling with another woman who was so tall and thin I thought she might blow away if the wind picked up.

Brandon was silently observing, then leaned over towards me and whispered, "Hey, I think if those two stood next to each other they would look like the number ten."

"Brandon!" I scolded, but he was already cackling at his own joke.

Well, the thin frail-looking one had a dog with her. It barked incessantly from the moment its paws hit the cold rocky shore, and it wasn't a normal bark either. It sounded like one of those screaming rubber chickens that squawked when you squeeze them. Everyone currently in the Hot Springs also was taking notice. The two women paid us no mind, and appeared to be getting back into their raft, when suddenly this small, disruptive, possibly handicapped dog caught sight of Jack. It did its best to run toward us, but the unstable slippery rocks made it difficult for its tiny paws. When it made it over to Jack, and I saw him close up, I had to hold back a giggle. It was the farthest thing from a river dog I had ever seen. (I realize that "river dog" is nowhere an official category for canines, but some breeds are more suited to water than others. When given the title, I imagine a dog with an athletic build, and a coat that's smooth and sleek like a Lab or long and shaggy like a Collie. Most importantly though, a strong swimmer) He belonged in a warm dry house and to be wearing a fancy collar in the lap of some sweet old lady. But in this case, he was wearing a doggie flotation vest with a handle on the back so his owner could pick him up and carry him like a suitcase. Which is what she did. She climbed over the slimy mossy rocks to retrieve him, but instead of walking back to her raft she picked up Scoop (I'm pretty sure that's what she called him, could have been Scoob too, but we're going with the first guess) and put him directly into the Hot Springs saying,

"Hello, I'm sure you all heard Scoop and I thought I would formally introduce him." As if to say, "sorry my dog is being annoying, let me just drop him in the middle of your fun as an apology." At least he had stopped barking, but only because he couldn't swim well, and his mouth was filling with water on each attempt. It was a pathetic sight to behold, and I reached out to try and steer his doggy paddle back to the shallow rocks. Glancing up at my original companions, I noticed Brandon and Rain were exchanging a goofy wide-eyed look.

Oh no, I thought. *It's kicking in.*

All of us agreed it was time to get out. Gingerly, we climbed over the wet rocks to towels and dry shoes. With one last look at Scoop cough-barking in the Hot Springs, we hiked back to our campsite. It was only a short distance away, but it felt like forever just to get back to our tents and hammocks. We all collapsed at the foot of a large spruce and stared quizzically at the leafy treetops. I had no idea what to expect, was I going to start seeing the canopy come to life? Were mysterious voices going to pop into my head? So far, I only felt slightly light-headed, like my body was standing up, but consciously I knew I was still sitting down. I glanced over at Rain who was sprawled out on the grass, perfect snow Angel position. He was gazing intently up towards the sky at something I could not see. I sighed loudly, disappointed that I wasn't feeling too different. I plucked a blade of grass from the dirt and turned my hand over to fiddle with it, but noticed that the creases on my palm were looking… not so normal….

Hoooooly shit they're moving! the voice in my head exclaimed.

Abruptly I brought my hand closer to my face for further observation and managed to smush my nose. Reeling back from my personal attack I looked down at the spot where I had just plucked the blade of grass, and noticed it was moving and swaying in an unnatural wave. Whoa.

This experience instantly accelerated. Everywhere I looked, if I fixated on one thing for longer than ten seconds, the image started to spin in a clockwise spiral. The trees were dancing in unison, the different shades of color on the rocky cliffs were waving back and forth to each other, keeping in step with the flow of the river. All I could do was stare off and get lost in the landscape around me. Standing up seemed very unnecessary, let alone walking. Besides, I now had to rediscover the complexity of the plants right in front of my eyes. So, for three hours we all settled in under that spruce tree, letting our minds wander to every level of our subconscious. I learned that when you're tripping, time seems to move uncommonly fast. So that three hours felt more like thirty minutes.

We could only imagine what our neighboring campers must have thought of us. They had walked by a few times and saw us lounging there in the same position under the tree. It wasn't until Jack woke up from his nap that we were pulled from our trance. He padded over to Brandon and laid his wet nose on his lap. He uttered a soft "woof" and then spun around in a tight circle, making a dust cloud on the ground. At first, I just watched the little dog, then within moments he became comedic. Like an unsuspecting hiccup, a laugh rose in my throat, and I couldn't stop it. Jack making his nest in the dirt was the funniest thing I had seen up to this point in my entire life. I had never (and still haven't) laughed so uncontrollably and unceasing. My outburst was shortly mimicked by Brandon and Trevor. The three of us were feeding off each other's hilarity in a contagious circle.

LSD typically lasts for eight to twelve hours. The high will come in waves, peaking and dropping up to three times during one trip. First comes the mind expansion, like you're seeing everything with new eyes. You feel like you're thinking with parts of your brain you have never used before. Then the slap-happy laughter fits. This part you just have to let happen; it's ridiculous, but there's no stopping it. Then you'll come down a bit, leading into an intellectual philosophy stage. This is when you'll become very insightful and wonder why you haven't thought of the world like this before. This was my favorite part of the trip.

It's true that the sober brain will "trick" you into seeing images that may not be their true form. Like subtle optical illusions that are constantly occurring. This method is how our brain intercepts what we see and tries to make sense of the world around us. It creates a diluted reality but makes life more easily navigable. On the third stage of an acid trip, this part of our mind is overruled, and you notice everything, even things that may or may not be there. Sounds become visible, light moves in a color spectrum of waves, and you realize how alive everything is, how it's all pulsing to the same beat.

The mind will cycle through these three stages, then repeat. We were still in stage two: none of us could manage to form a sentence, eye contact alone that prompted another giggle fest. Just when we began to come down and catch our breath, our neighbors walked by with their dog on a leash. We didn't want to appear too suspicious, so we quickly looked away from each other and tried to act like we weren't tripping our asses off. We maintained composure long enough for them to almost be out of earshot. Then Brandon opened his mouth.

Apparently, he had spoken to this couple when we first arrived at Radium and learned that their dog had recently been neutered, which was why they were keeping him on a leash. Nobody else knew of this conversation, so we were slightly dumbfounded when Brandon shouted, "Sorry about your nuts man!"

I didn't know which was funnier, the genuine sincerity on Brandon's face or the utter confusion of the dog's owners. Appearing normal after this was a lost cause. We gave in to the chemicals and didn't stop laughing until our sides ached and tears were running down our faces.

After this the hysteria started to subside, and our minds expanded deeper into thought. Philosophical stage three. We we're sprawled out on the grass watching the tree canopy's twirl in a kaleidoscope fashion, when a branch snapped nearby, and I heard dried grass crunching under foot. A figure approached from up the hill, and I rolled over onto my stomach to see Rain standing alone, gazing out over the far embankment.

"Whatcha thinking about?" I managed to say.

"I lost my hammock," he said.

"Oh...?" I questioned with a raised eyebrow. His hammock was still hanging exactly where he left it in plain sight.

"It's right over there." I pointed to the spruce behind him. Slowly he turned, and without further communication, climbed into his hammock and succumbed to his thoughts. Turning back to look at the river, I noticed Trevor and Brandon were gone. Walking seemed more doable now, so I strolled down to the riverbank.

It was a steep trail, so I watched my feet the entire descent, making sure not to fall over any exposed roots or loose rocks. When I got down to the water and really saw the river, I began to feel the strength of my trip again. There was an old-looking hemlock stretching out over the water, creating a pleasant shaded spot on the sand. The invitation was too perfect, so I went over and plopped down cross-legged on the cool ground and watched the running water splash and flow freely over the stones on the bank.

A shadow crossed in front of my bare feet, and I looked up to see an eagle soaring overhead. I thought about the acuteness of their senses and imagined they might be similar to mine at the moment. Everything was so crystal clear, like a live action 4K *Planet Earth* episode. I couldn't tell you how many times prior to this I had just sat and listened to nature, but this was a new kind of surround sound. I lay back, resting my head on the large boulder under the tree.

I should take a picture, I thought. I knew the photo would not do justice to the feeling, but it would prompt a memory. Holding my phone up I snapped a shot of the river with the bank rising up to the grassy hills on the other side. The shutter sound from my phone camera birthed an idea that took me on a very intricate train of thought.

Everyone takes pictures. Everyone wants to capture certain moments in time to remember forever. Photography involves so much more than a camera and nice scenery though. Professional photographers plan, travel, hike, and wait sometimes for long stretches of time, just to get that perfect shot, to click at the right moment, at a specific angle with proper lighting. Patience plays a huge role in capturing that photo. But what we as readers and photo lovers see, is only what the photographer wants us to see. What about the rest of the landscape outside the frame? What would we see if they had moved slightly to the left?

I imagined being a photographer in the moment after the camera click. Freezing their view through the lens forever, then looking up from the tripod and turning to marvel at the rest of the world around them. What they saw then, we'll never know. This is what went through my brain after snapping that picture on my Samsung.

Because of that afternoon I have a better appreciation for photographers. Even now, writing this book, years later and not on hallucinogens, I can still see the passing shadow of that eagle and feel vividly that same wonder.

My river pondering was interrupted by Trevor and Brandon scrambling down from the ledge above my hemlock. Rocks slid and tumbled down next to me followed by the thud of their bare feet on the sand. The boys smiled and asked if they should start collecting wood for a fire.

Was it already that late? The afternoon had flown by, sure enough I looked to the clouds and saw they were turning shades of pink and orange. In the setting sun, our trip was coming to a close. I could feel my mind retracting, returning to normality. My thoughts were quieter, and I could focus longer on completing a task (like collecting firewood). The night ended with everyone retiring to their vessels of sleep. I felt like I had just taken back-to-back final exams. My brain was exhausted but contently so. This was a day I will never forget.

~...~...~

Chapter 11
About Progress

With winter coming to a close, my job at Winter Park was almost finished for the season. This meant that if I wanted to keep getting paid, I had to find a new job. Brandon told Trevor and I that the place he worked at was hiring and encouraged us to apply. This was a rustic, beautiful mountain resort called Devils Thumb Ranch Resort and Spa. Just a fifteen-minute commute from our apartment, nestled in a gorgeous valley behind Winter Park, off County road 83. I had been living here in the Valley for over a year now and didn't know this place even existed, but it seemed like an elite establishment from their website, and there was an opening in the culinary department. To spare you the details. I applied, got an interview, and soon enough I was hired on as a chef at Ranch House, Devils Thumbs fine-dining restaurant.

Trevor and Rain were also successful in getting a job at Devils Thumb Ranch. Rain was hired on in catering, and Trevor would help manage the front desk. But before starting work, we were going to go back to Illinois for my brother's eighth grade graduation. It was a short trip, but also my first time being home since moving, so I was a little nervous, and excited to see family again. This would also be the first time seeing my mom and dad since I had written them my letter. I knew they had received and read it, but there had been no following discussion. Before our plane landed, I decided I wasn't going to be the one to bring it up. I had said everything I needed. Metaphorically the ball was now in their court.

At the airport they appeared happy to see Trevor and I. Jonathan had grown at least a foot since the last time I saw him, but his hug was the best to come home to.

It's difficult connecting sometimes when you are eight years apart from your sibling; as he got older though, Jonathan and I were slowly becoming closer. Like me, he went to Catholic grade school, so those of you who can relate will understand when I say it was a short church service. There were six students in his graduating class, and they all looked so proud standing up there in front of the congregation in their royal blue caps and gowns. It was a lovely morning filled with old friends, followed by a delicious brunch back at my parents' house, carefully catered by yours truly. One of the perks of coming home is that there's always a delicious spread of food. That evening Trevor and I were sitting on the porch swing, discussing the bonfire we were attending later that night. Jonathan was inside counting the wad of graduation cash he had received for the fourth time, when my dad came out and sat on the top porch step. He had been rather quiet since my return. I knew his mind was working hard, but I doubted there would be any real conversation. Trevor stood up from the swing and asked if I was ready to head out.

"Yeah sure," I responded, "just let me find a jacket."

He hopped down the steps in his flip-flops to the car to wait for me. I stepped inside to grab one of my mom's jackets (all of mine were still in Colorado) I poked my head out the door to tell my dad I was leaving.

"Okay, where are you going?" he asked.

"Just over to Cody's for a fire." (Cody was/is my cousin and good friend who lived roughly twenty miles away)

"Oh, all right, well, have fun." He didn't even turn around to look at me. But, before I had let go of the doorknob, my dad stopped me,

"Wait, Natalie," I heard him say.

I stepped back onto the porch, one foot inside, hand still on the door.

"Yes?" I said.

He stood up and turned to face me. "Can I have a hug before you leave?"

"Oh... um, yeah okay," I said. Reflecting back, I wish I hadn't sounded so perplexed. A hug from your father shouldn't be something to question.

Stepping out onto the porch, I let the screen door slam behind me and went to hug the man for the first time in a while. He wrapped his arms around me and held on tightly. I knew he needed this and had probably been feeling a little helpless since his visit to Winter Park. I laid my head against his chest and hugged him back. His coat smelled like grass clippings and laundry detergent. A scent I had associated with him my entire life. They say smells can trigger the strongest memories, and in that brief moment I felt an old familiar sense of security. Growing up, I felt this all the time. Going for bike rides, fishing trips, days at my grandparent's lake, were times that at any moment I could turn to see my dad standing not far off. He wasn't always watching or paying close attention, but I knew he was there. And because of that, my small world was all right. Pulling back from the embrace on the porch I smiled up at him and was caught off guard to see a tear in his eye. I could count on two fingers the number of times I had seen my dad cry, and this was the second.

"I'm really glad you're home," he said. I didn't know what to do.

"Well, I'm glad too" was all I could think of.

"I know we don't see eye to eye on a lot of things," he said, "but the last thing I want is for you to feel like we aren't proud of you, because your mother and I are both very proud of the young woman you are becoming."

"Wow…," I murmured. "Thanks for saying so."

He continued. "I know you're going to live differently than your mom and I, I'm just going to learn to accept it. We only want the absolute best for you, Natalie, because we love you. One day, if you are a parent, you will understand."

I had temporarily forgotten how to speak, so I just looked at him admiringly for a moment. When words came back, I just replied, "I love you too. It means a lot to hear you say that… really, it does."

"Well, I won't keep you. Have a good time at your fire." And just like that, the moment was over, but as I slipped my arms through the sleeve of the jacket, I couldn't help grinning. A weight had been lifted, and I felt a swift rush of relief knowing that my parents and I, especially my dad, would be able to reconnect. I knew there would still be disagreements and the occasional stern look from across the dinner table, but navigating adulthood while keeping a close relationship with your parents is a process that takes compromise from both sides. We had been falling short since I moved out, but walking to Trevor waiting in the car that night, I felt confident that we were back on track again.

~…~…~

Chapter 12
About a Mountain

That summer in Colorado, similar to the first winter, held many life changes. I began working for Devils Thumb Ranch at Ranch House Restaurant, I climbed a mountain, I saw on Alpine Lake, I bought a mountain bike—the list goes on. To tell you about it all would take another novel; I could write a hundred more pages just on my experiences as a chef at Ranch House. The restaurant life, front of house and back of house, is a world of its own. (Who knows? Maybe I will someday.) But this book is not about work.

Trevor and I went on numerous outdoor adventures throughout the season. We arranged our schedules so that we always had one, sometimes two, days off together. We took advantage of these days to go on hikes, bike rides, picnics, anything that would take us out into the Colorado wilderness, away from the fast-paced work grind. One of the more monumental hikes was Byers Peak. Standing at 12,84 feet in elevation, Byers loomed in the distance behind our apartment. We saw it every day, and the call to summit it grew with every glance, until finally the day came when we shouldered our backpacks, complete with snacks (mostly on Trevor's part, I always forget to bring snacks), plenty of water, a hammock and snowshoes. The peak wasn't completely melted yet, and I wasn't about to trudge through snow drifts in my KEENs. We drove ten miles over a dirt road that turned into a very rough and narrow rocky lane, eventually arriving at the trailhead. A light brown National Park Service sign read, in the iconic yellow painted letters, "Byers Peak Wilderness." We parked the Escape, signed our names in the hiker's log and set out.

The first two miles was a wide gravel service road that wound up and around through the woods. It ended at a footbridge that crossed over St. Louis

Creek to a dirt path that we would stay on to the top. Aspen and Cedar groves bordered the trail. The trees had all sorts of twisted trunks and slumping branches. Trevor found one that had a root sticking out of the ground in the shape of a recliner chair. So of course, we had to stop for a photo opp. Walking through the woods I let my mind drift away from my footsteps and settle on the sounds of the creek below. The water flowed over smooth pebbles, splashing about the fallen logs, and gurgling in a slow current around the pools formed by beaver dams. Birds chirped back and forth to each other, probably complaining about the mischievous red squirrels scurrying about the higher branches.

We hiked at a good clip, with Trevor in the lead. Our water breaks were strategically placed so that when we stopped, there was a gap in the trees. We could rehydrate while taking in the view of Byers peak growing ever closer. As we climber higher, the trees gradually began to get shorter and more spread out, letting in more sunlight to dry out the wet ground. With the quickly approaching tree line, the trail grew steeper and more strenuous. The elevation change was also making our breathing come in shallower breaths. My throat started to burn from the sharp inhales, and my head began to spin slightly. Since arriving in Colorado, the altitude hadn't had a negative effect on me until now.

Emerging from the protection of the Aspens, out on to the open mountainside, the wind hit us in full force. Hiking up from the bottom with nothing but a faint breeze and ample sunshine, we had worked up a sweat, dampening our clothes. This made the brisk wind bite a little harder. Ahead I could see where the pale brown and sparse green of dried grass turned to hard packed silvery snow. We stopped at the edge of the frosted field and slipped snowshoes on over our hiking footwear. Trekking over the crunchy surface, we took high-kneed steps, and carefully placed each footfall to avoid breaking through a soft patch to a hidden hole. Despite our efforts, we did fall into an unseen pocket that left us in thigh-high powder. No harm done, though. After another half mile, we arrived at the end of the snowfield. We were high enough now on the mountain where the wind was too gusty for snow to stick. Any new dusting in the last month had simply blown away. The snowshoes were convenient, but I was happy to unstrap and leave them behind for the remainder of the hike. There was a lone scraggly bush off to the left of the trail, so we stashed our snowshoes under the low branches and continued along a narrow ridge.

With most mountain hikes, at some point close to the top, the trail will turn to scree (loose and broken rock fragments) turning the hike into a precarious scramble. It can also make the route slightly unclear.

This happened to Trevor and I. When we approached large granite boulders jutting out of the ground, Trevor climbed over them as I'd imagine a mountain goat would, quick and nimble without wavering, which irked me because I took my time making sure not to slip and gouge my knee on a pointed rock. Once over this obstacle, the incline steepened, and I stared crestfallen at the remaining walk in front of me. This last stretch felt the longest, but I couldn't catch my breath. Trevor may already have been at the summit for all I knew. I was just focusing on not passing out 12,000-plus feet up on the spine of a mountain. Finally though dragging my feet and attempting to stop wheezing, I stepped onto the summit.

Praise God, I thought to myself. Trevor came running over, and I collapsed in an exhausted heap. He sat down next to me and with one arm pulled me onto his lap.

"We did it!" he shouted into the wind.

I high-fived his upheld hand and smiled at the pride beaming from his face. In the lenses of the aviator's he was wearing, I could see the reflection of the mountains beyond. My legs were burning, my feet were cold, and my throat could use a lozenge, but I was so proud of our accomplishment. For the first time in my young life, I was standing on top of a mountain. Taking in the view, all physical pain was forgotten. I was speechless. The Rockies stretched on forever, the topography falling and rising from one peak to the next. The lakes below us now looked like small ponds, puddle-like, and St. Louis Creek a gentle stream. I could have stared, wonderstruck, at that horizon forever.

While holding my phone up to take a picture, Trevor snuck up from behind and gave me a bear hug. Startled, I nearly dropped my phone, but he just laughed and pulled me closer. I rested my arms on top of his around my waist and leaned back against him. Together we stood on Byer's Peak, looking out over the stunning Colorado wilderness. Some folks have to travel hundreds of miles to get views like this, and here I was with a magical valley right in my backyard. I felt blessed to call this small section of The Rockies home. On that day, on that rugged peak, my heart swelled. In my admiration, I realized I'd fallen head over heels in love with those mountains.

Chapter 13
About Growing Pains

Every adventure we went on that summer was memorable in its own way. From the top of that mountain to hidden gems nestled in the interior of Rocky Mountain National Park. The raw beauty of Momma Nature continued to humble me. I wanted to share the emotions these journeys evoked with my friends back in Illinois, but the more I saw of the world out here, the further detached I became from the people I grew up with. My second trip back to visit my family showed me just how distant.

Trevor and I were headed back to southern Illinois to celebrate our good friends Chris and Kelly's wedding. Our new friends we had in Colorado were wonderful, but nothing compared with returning to our old stomping grounds and getting the squad back together. Needless to say, we were both excited.

The morning of the wedding I woke up in my old bedroom at my parents' house and was happy to make breakfast in a kitchen big enough to accommodate more than three people. Apartment living had given me a respect for average sized houses. After a delicious stack of pancakes, I started getting ready for the afternoon. My dress was a solid color, hot pink with half shoulder sleeves and a shallow crew neckline. It fit snugly down to my waist, then flared out loosely to a hem just above my knees. There were straps crisscrossing up the back, which gave it a hint of sensuality but still acceptable to wear to the church.

When Trevor and I walked in to take our seats for the service, we watched polite smiles on our friends faces turn to genuine excitement as they realized their long-lost companions from the Rockies had returned. We were met with so many hugs and "we miss yous." My heart was full of the warm welcomes we had received. It felt as if we had never left.

Despite all the good vibes and pleas to move back to Illinois, being in the community I grew up in made me realize something. While Trevor and I were tackling life in Colorado, everything here seemed to stay the same. Driving into town that afternoon I saw the same cars, parked in the same spots, outside the same bars and restaurants from when I left. The grocery store sign still had the same light out. The sidewalk outside the bank had the same crack with dandelions poking through, and at the Phillips 66, I was greeted by the same face of the eccentric cashier, wearing another bright floral button-up. As if on cue he asked if I would like a box of junior mints, to which I replied as I always had, "Not this time, Pete, just filling up."

The nice old man who walks his dog twice a day down Main Street from the Dairy Queen to Ace Hardware was there, shuffling along at his slow pace. It felt like the town was one big clock, each building representing a number. All the people were living their everyday life around the same gears, just ticking routinely away. When I had left months ago on that October afternoon, the DQ sign read "Blizzard of the month: Sea Salt Truffle" now it read "S'mores." Other than that, and maybe a new coat of paint on the elementary school, nothing had changed. I saw from a new perspective how simple my childhood home was. This wasn't a bad feeling though. I loved my childhood. No, this realization was more of a reassurance that I had made the right decision to move out West.

I didn't miss the places as much as I missed the people here. If only I could bring all my loved ones with me on my adventures, then it would be perfect. Leaving was always hard. I didn't know when I would see those friends again. In those moments, when I'm closing the car door and looking up into the rearview to see sad faces waving back at me, for a fleeting second, I think, *I'm not leaving. I have to stay.* But deep down I knew I would only grow restless in this Midwest town. Goodbyes were tough, but I knew those wonderful people would still be there when I returned, whenever that may be.

~...~...~

Back in Fraser, work life was running smoothly, but my time at home with Trevor seemed to be moving in a different direction, with increasing hours and opposite work schedules, we had little time to spend with each other. Most days I would come home from a long shift to find him asleep on the couch, or I would wake up alone because he had to be at work by 6:00 A.M. Parallel to the rough patch we went through when we first moved out, there wasn't any one thing either of us was doing wrong, we just were not making any effort to spend time together. After a while we began to drift apart again. I started to take little snide remarks Trevor would say and turn them into a something they weren't. My patience with him shortened because I thought he had no desire to make time for me. Trevor is not a very emotional person, so talking about feelings doesn't come willingly. I came to the conclusion that if he didn't want to talk, then I wasn't going to try. So, there we were again, going about our day acting more like siblings than a couple.

Truthfully, I hated it. I wanted so bad to just curl up in his lap, kiss his sweet face and stay awake laughing and talking all night like we used to. But to my irrational pride that would mean that I lost whatever game we were playing. So instead I acted like everything was fine, that I didn't have a care in the world if Trevor went off mountain biking for hours and didn't tell me. No worries if we didn't talk to each other all day. I just brushed all negative feelings aside. But as more time passed the silent tension between us grew. Trevor kept his emotional doors closed, and I didn't make any efforts to open them.

To keep the metaphors rolling, the issue here is that I'm an open book. I needed to voice things with another to solve problems. And if Trevor wasn't going to talk, I would find another. The people I was closest to here in the valley were my coworkers, and while we were all good friends, I doubted they would have the time or sympathy for my relationship woes. That left me with one other option. The only person besides Trevor who really was there all the time, listening, laughing, and living in the room next door. Rain.

~...~...~

One of the traits I valued most about Rain was that he was very emotionally understanding. He connected well with his own feelings, and the two of us had many in-depth conversations about his past, and the hardships he endured growing up. I listened while he told me about his inner vices, and when I needed it, he listened to me too. We became a kind of confidant to each other, which in turn strengthened our already close friendship.

Besides sharing an apartment, Rain and I had the same schedule, so we frequently found ourselves the only two at the kitchen table, or watching Netflix in the game room. The more time we shared, the more we talked, and the more intimate those conversations became.

He listened intently when I told him about the strain on my and Trevor's relationship and offered what advice he could. If he didn't have an answer, he would say or do something to try and make me feel better, and most of the time it did.

The weight on Trevor and I lifted slightly, but only because I had someone else who reciprocated my emotional energy; therefore, I was less stressed, more laid-back. Things were simple and easy between us. Meanwhile Rain and I had become not just roommates, but best friends.

Could I maintain my relationship with Trevor and keep my friendship with Rain though? That thought hadn't crossed my mind until the night we held a fall bonfire at our apartment. That was when things started to slip out of my control.

~…~…~

Chapter 14
About Boundaries

As previously stated, we had a decent-sized yard with a firepit, back deck, and a full-sized grill. There was a small group of friends and neighbors over, music was playing, a fire was blazing, and most of the party was on their third or fourth drink, myself included. Trevor and Brandon were standing out front having what seemed to be a very serious conversation about mountain biking, and I had just stepped back outside after putting another layer on. Hearing the intensity in their voices, I knew any attempt to sway their attention would be useless. A group had recently left on a beer run, leaving Rain sitting alone on a stump by the fire. Casually I strolled over to join him. The smoke was blowing toward the apartment, so I went to slide in-between him and the fence to the chair on the other side. The gap wasn't very big, so I turned sideways to squeeze through. Putting my hands on his shoulders for balance I side-stepped behind him to the chair on the other side. After sitting down, I realized I was closer to him than the placement of the chair led me to believe. Our legs touched momentarily and for a fleeting second, I felt a prickling sensation roll over my entire body, with a heat that had little to do with the fire.

Whoa, I thought. We made eye contact, and I let my gaze linger before picking up my chair and scooting a few feet away. I took another long pull from my cider and thought, *I'm going to ignore that, it was nothing*.

But as everyone knows you can't simply ignore those kinds of feelings. It's like wildfire: once there's a spark, if you don't acknowledge and extinguish it, it will grow.

But you're with Trevor, Natalie. You love Trevor, I told myself. Which was very true, we may have communication issues, but I loved that boy.

Was I developing feelings beyond friendship for Rain?

Jesus Christ, girl, my inner monologue ridiculed me.

Thankfully the return of our friends from the beer store pulled me out of my head. The group around the fire grew full again. Trevor walked over and put his arm around me. Rain remained fairly quiet but seemed content. I laughed with the rest of them, and the night carried on. But the feeling of that sudden rush lingered in my chest. I told myself it was the alcohol, but deep down I knew it was something much more.

~...~...~

Earlier that summer Rain, Trevor, and I discussed the possibility of us going on a fall trip together. October marked the end of the busy season at DTR. Rain and I had similar weeks off, so once we chose a date, all Trevor had to do was request off himself.

We decided it would be fun to go somewhere that wasn't in the mountains, and hopefully had temperatures higher than sixty degrees. Rain hadn't been home to Florida in a few years. Plus, he had some old friends in Louisiana he wanted to visit. He assured us he could get a place for us all to stay if Trevor and I could provide a vehicle. It was gearing up to be the perfect road trip.

We planned on heading south at the close of the season. A date was set, itineraries were made, all that was left was the waiting.

In the meantime though, things had changed between Trevor, Rain and I. At the end of our lease, he (Rain) moved into employee housing through DTR to take an RA position in one of the lodges. There were no hard feelings involved, quite the opposite. It was simply a good financial opportunity for him. Trevor and I stayed in the same building but downsized to the single bedroom unit. I was a little averse to it at first because it would be so much smaller, but was pleasantly surprised at how much I liked living there once we moved in.

The new living arrangements meant Trevor and I would have more time just the two of us. At first it was wonderful. We started having long talks again, making dinner together, just like our first apartment. Soon, though, I started to miss Rain. I had gotten so used to him always being there. Now when Trevor and I had conflicting schedules (which still was often) it was just me at the apartment. I found myself frequently stopping by the employee lodge after work to hang out with

Rain and other coworkers who shared my night shift before going home. And on one such evening, after sharing a bowl (not the kind with cereal and milk) between three people, I was walking to my car, but stopped when I noticed the motion light flick on. Turning around I saw Rain in the driveway, and for a moment just stared at his figure, his face shadowed by the dim lighting. He walked over and stood next me, leaning against my car, his hands in his pockets.

"I miss you, Rain," I said softly

"I miss you too, Natalie," he said back. There was a pause, and I thought I heard faint music. Then I noticed he had ear buds hanging from his coat, and the song that was playing was one I had sent him.

"Hey, isn't that a song I sent you?" I asked, knowing already that it was.

"Yea it is." I could see a smile under his hood.

The song was "I'll Find You" by Tori Kelly. Part of the refrain goes like this:

> *Just fight a little longer, my friend*
> *It's all worth it in the end*
> *But when you got nobody to turn to*
> *Just hold on and I'll find you*

"That entire song really hit home for me, ya know?" he said quietly.

"Well, you know the reasons I sent it. Think of the lyrics as a message from me to you. And no matter what, I'll always be here to help in whatever way I can, even if it's just listening."

"Thank you…," he replied in barely a whisper. "Nobody has ever said something like that to me before; I've never been a person someone wants to care for that much."

"I'm just telling the truth." And indeed, I was.

Before saying goodnight, I opened my arms to him. Out there in the dim light from the employee lodge, under the stars he held on to me, and in his embrace, there was more than a friendly hug, there was a longing, a desire. I felt it in the pressure of his arms around my waist. Stepping back into the shadow of the doorway, the tips of his fingers grazed mine, and he looked up at me with an adoration I will always remember. In that one moment, however brief, Rain was truly happy, there was a joy in his eyes that almost brought tears to my own.

On the drive home that night, I thought of our beach vacation quickly approaching and whether or not it would still be a good idea. Rain clearly had feelings for me, and I'd be lying if I said I didn't have some toward him too, and it was getting harder to keep them at bay. I wasn't doing anything to stop them from developing further either. No, I was just continuing down this slippery slope, living in two different worlds, two separate relationships. One with Trevor that was openly known to everyone, safe and secure. And the other with Rain, fueled on emotion, secrecy, and a little mystery. The fine line of "just friends" was getting harder to keep my balance on.

~...~...~

Chapter 15
About Florida

Then something happened that launched me further into my predicament. Trevor told me he wasn't going on the trip.

"WHAT?! Seriously?" I shouted when he told me the news. "We've been talking about this for over a month! Rain already has places for us to stay!"

"I know, I know," he said from behind the counter. "I just forgot to ask off in time."

"You just forgot to ask off in time…," I repeated. I was glad there was a counter between us at the moment.

"Well, that's not a good enough excuse. I reminded you SEVERAL times, and you said you would do it two weeks ago. Now what are we supposed to do?" I demanded.

"I'm sorry. I know I fucked up, but there's nothing I can do to get those days off now, you and Rain just go without me," he said.

"Ugh!" I needed a minute to calm down before I could attempt to figure anything out. Slamming my hands down on the counter I walked out on the deck, silently thankful that the cup in my hand wasn't glass.

Now my already flustered mind was tainted with anger. Not the best mix for good decisions making. Anyhow, I decided that Trevor or no Trevor I was going on the trip. It had been a long exhausting summer in the DTR kitchen, and I needed a break, so what if it was just going to be me and Rain. Besides, Trevor did say we should still go, that means he's okay with it, right?

~…~…~

The last night at Ranch House Restaurant before break, we had an exceptionally delicious, extra fancy staff dinner to celebrate a successful busy season. Once it was finished, I clocked out, drove straight to the lodge, picked up Rain, popped an Adderall to stay awake, and headed up and over Berthoud pass on our journey to warmer weather.

During the drive south to Florida, Rain and I took turns driving. When we weren't listening to music or a podcast, our time was filled with constant conversation. The two-day road trip felt like no time at all, and soon we were pulling into the driveway of his friend's beach house. I opened the passenger door, stepped out into the light from the setting sun and inhaled deeply, letting the cool evening air fill my lungs. There was a warm breeze blowing up off the ocean, and unlike in Colorado, I could look out over the horizon and see forever. That endless skyline was incredibly beautiful. As we carried our things inside, I stopped for a moment on the front porch and just gazed out to the open water, the colors from the clouds were reflecting off the ocean in glittery oranges, reds, and subtle pinks. I smiled and thought to myself, *Damn…I love the beach.*

Rain's friend Tommy was gracious enough to let us stay with him in his gorgeous three-story beach house. We spent the first two days exploring their old neighborhoods, dining on phenomenal sea food, and dozing on sandy towels in the hot October sun. I felt like I was in a lazy dream. But our most important reason for coming to Panama City Beach was to meet with Rain's mother. He hadn't seen her or his little sister in years, and the fact he wanted me present for their reunion meant a lot.

We met them outside a Mexican restaurant where we were going to have lunch. When they saw each other across the parking lot, his mom's eyes lit up, and she ran over to hug her son. I hung back at first to give them a moment alone, and to let Rain get reacquainted with his little sister. After the heartfelt hellos had been said, and I had been introduced, we went inside to eat. The afternoon was spent telling stories, hearing new ones, and listening to Rain's little sister tell us about preschool and all her new friends. His mom was enthralled with everything he had to say, from kitchen work to the snowy slopes. I could see how much she adored him, and how he cared for her too. I saw a gentle, tender, almost nurturing side of Rain that he'd kept hidden before.

Sitting there at the table I wondered what it must be like to have so much time go by without seeing a parent or a child. I know it's a reality for many people, but it was never for me. Until recently my entire family (immediate and extended) had always been an hour's drive away. I was beginning to understand how very different our lives were, Rain and I. We thought the same and enjoyed many of the same things, but he grew up with hardships I will never know. I was developing a new sense of appreciation for him. His walls were breaking down to expose a deeply scarred but very loving heart.

~...~...~

While sweet, the days in Florida were short-lived. The last afternoon was spent at multiple car dealerships. Vehicles here were much cheaper here than in Colorado, and Rain was tired of relying on friends to give him a ride everywhere. As most endeavors like these go, it took longer than anticipated with unforeseen obstacles. However, after many phone calls, signatures, credit checks, and loan approvals, Rain drove off the lot with his very own Subaru Forester.

So far, we were enjoying each other's company just as any two friends would. Side by side, yet with a safe distance. Sleeping in our own rooms, but still ignoring the ever-present tension humming between us.

Chapter 16
About New Orleans

It wasn't until Louisiana that things started to get interesting, and by interesting, I mean I got myself into trouble. Rain had lived in New Orleans for the first thirteen years of his life, after junior high, his mom moved them to Florida. Because we were only three hours away, we decided to stop and hopefully meet up with some of the folks he grew up with. It also happened to be October 30, the day before All Hallows Eve. Rain got in touch with his friend Dillion, who invited us to a Halloween party. We didn't have any costumes but still happily said yes to the invitation. When we arrived, I thought to myself, *These people are just like my own small-town friends.* Everyone was welcoming and very eager to bring us into the crowd loosely circling the bonfire and to show us around the spookily decorated house. We were treated by the hosts as if we had hung out every weekend together.

So once again Rain's friends provided a place for us to stay. This time it was simply a couch and pull-out mattress at Dillion's apartment he shared with his girlfriend Kayla. Southern hospitality wouldn't allow us to sleep at a hotel. I felt at home amongst these kind people and looked forward to the following night on the New Orleans strip.

I woke the next morning a little stiff from sleeping in one position all night on a couch that was slightly too short for me, but otherwise in great spirits. Everyone else was still in bed, so I got up quietly, went out to the car and drove into town to get coffee for myself and our hosts. When I returned no one had stirred from their slumber so I patiently waited, reading a book I had brought along, until I heard sounds of movement from the room next to me. Eventually, three sleepy-eyed friends shuffled out to say good morning and start the day.

Our afternoon began with a tour of all their favorite places. Then we went to lunch at a dive bar right across from Café Du Monde. The bartender running the place was also the only waitress. She looked like a young schoolteacher but had the attitude of a prison guard and cursed like a sailor. I felt like I was back in the kitchen instead of sitting in the dining room. I loved it. Plus, the food was great, and the clientele sitting at the bar watching a football game kept us thoroughly entertained.

After lunch we visited the aquarium. Growing up in the St. Louis area, aquariums weren't exactly popular, so getting to see the one in New Orleans was a real treat.

Every exhibit was a floor-to-ceiling tank filled with colorful tropical fish from the reefs of Australia to the wild waters of the Amazon. We explored for nearly two hours before leaving to head back downtown. As we walked out the exit door, Rain stopped and asked if we could take a picture together. He gave his phone to Dillion, then walked over, put his arm around me and said, "This is such a good day; I want to remember it." With a big smile we turned to the camera and laughed at Dillion who was making a goofy face while holding up the phone.

"Say cheeeeeese," he shouted.

I can still hear the shutter sound and can still remember squinting from the sun glinting off the rim of Rain's glasses.

~...~...~

There was a party on Bourbon Street that night, and we were going with Dillion and Kayla. They said we hadn't experienced Halloween until we had survived the New Orleans version of it.

Survived? I had thought. *What exactly are we getting ourselves into?*

I soon found out and was not disappointed. Walking down the sidewalk just before dusk, Rain and I kept a quick pace trying to keep up with our friends. Kayla was so excited she started skipping, saying she couldn't wait for the multiple parties to start and for us to witness them. I hadn't ever been to a street party, but I'd watched some movies, seen on social media and just heard through the grapevine that they were the wildest of celebrations.

The music could be heard from four blocks away. It was nearly nightfall, and I looked up to the horizon right as the last wisp of blue/gray light disappeared and gave way to the full blackness of a starry sky. A few minutes later, we turned and entered the lively street that was already buzzing with energy and overflowing with people in all variety of costume. Pale yellow light from the streetlamps mingled with the fluorescent red, green, and blue neon flashing in the shop windows. Rain, Dillion, Kayla, and I marveled at the lavishly decorated balconies and storefronts. Street performers sat at every other corner. Some were playing upside-down five-gallon buckets as drums. Others were break dancing under the streetlamps, adorned with flashing colored necklaces that threw trippy shadows up the sides of the buildings.

Kayla pulled us into a voodoo shop and began thumbing through a deck of tarot cards. I followed a bit cautiously behind her. Voodoo shops were another business not typically found near my hometown. Most folks considered it the hobby of heathens, but curiosity won over my conscience. Each wall had its own shrine covered with signs warning us not to touch or take any kind of photo. The main entrance led into what looked like a gift shop with books, cards, masks, costumes, and other souvenir-like trinkets. But at the far corner there was a long black curtain concealing a doorway. I zigzagged my way over and pulled back the curtain to peek around the frame and was surprised to find a whole additional shop! This one felt more authentic, like here was where all the good stuff was hidden. The shrines were bigger and more heavily adorned. There were locks and chains across the bookshelves. In front of the counter was a glass case filled with ingredients for spell casting and potion making. I felt a hand on my shoulder and jumped. Then exhaled a quiet sigh of relief to see it was Rain.

"What are you doing?" he whispered.

"I want to check this out real quick," I replied.

I could tell Rain wasn't too sure about it, but he followed me in behind the curtain. There were significantly less people on this side of the shop. They each seemed to be consumed with their own matter of business, not looking up or turning their heads at us newcomers. What really caught my attention were the books. Lining the entire far wall were volumes and volumes of genuine spell books. I walked over to the counter and rang the bell. A small hooded man came slinking around from one of the shelves, and when he took off his hood, I had to hold back a gasp. He had the smallest head of any grown man I'd ever seen. Being in a voodoo shop with my wild imagination I thought to myself, *I wonder what he did to piss off a witch and get cursed with a tiny head?*

"Can I help you?" he said in a low gravelly voice.

"Oh... I... um, yeah just wanted to look at one of those books on the shelf behind you; that one specifically."

I pointed to a red leather-bound book that had the title embroidered in gold thread on its binding. It read *Magic Through the Ages*.

The man looked at the book, then back at me, paused, then asked what category of spell I was wanting to attempt. His question was unexpected.

"Oh, well I don't have one in particular. I just really like books and wanted to thumb through its pages." My answer didn't faze him. He remained expressionless and unblinking.

"Well, I'm afraid I can't help you; only serious spell casters are allowed to peruse the pages of these manuscripts."

Manuscripts, I thought. *Is he a paid actor? Or is this for real?*

The hair standing up on the back of my neck told me, real or not, it was time to rejoin the party, and leave this creepy shop within a shop. Which we did. I thanked the man with the tiny head anyway, then Rain and I slipped back to the other side of the curtain to look for our friends. We found them in line to buy a T-shirt and a small glass bowl.

While waiting, I peered into the long cases holding all manner of smoking pipes, bowls, hookahs, and other ornate glass pieces. I had no intention of buying anything, but up on the highest shelves, above all the glass was an assortment of wooden pieces. They were beautiful. Intricately hand-carved sculptures, from dragons to wizards to miniature willow trees. One in particular caught my eye; it was pipe with a thin stem and the head of an owl carved onto the bowl. It was resting precariously on the edge of the shelf and looked just big enough to fit in the palm of my hand. A woman working behind the counter walked over to the shelf, and without saying a word, reached up, took down the owl pipe and handed it to me. There was a store full of people all talking and waiting to be checked out. Meanwhile I hadn't said anything to this woman indicating I wanted that pipe. In fact, I hadn't said anything at all. How did she know? I looked up at her surprisingly puzzled. She just smiled, patted my hand and said, "This one was made for you." Then went back to attending the other customers.

I couldn't not buy it now. So, I stood in line with the rest. Maybe this was a tactic of hers to get people to buy things, to just hand them a product and tell them it was fate. But still, meant to be or not that owl pipe was the one thing in that store I thought about purchasing. Walking out I glanced back at the woman and she winked at me.

Weird.

If I was in different circumstances, I would have found a quiet place to study that owl pipe and think more about my odd experience in the voodoo shop. But this was Halloween, and I was on Bourbon Street in New Orleans. Kayla must have noticed I was getting lost in my own thoughts and pulled me out of them.

"Hey, daydreamer!" she yelled from the middle of the street. "You like to dance?" As she said this, she attempted a ballerina twirl and almost knocked the drink out of the hand of a passerby.

The four of us laughed.

"I thought you'd never ask!" I shouted back over the music.

"Yeeeeeee-haw!" she exclaimed, bounding off down the street shouting for us to follow.

Kayla weaved in and out of the crowd, Dillion, Rain and I closely in tow to what she said was her favorite karaoke bar in Louisiana.

"There's usually five people up on stage at a time, then at 10:00 P.M. the whole place turns into a dance club," she told us excitedly.

I too was excited at the prospect of dancing. It's one of my favorite pastimes. Whenever I'm home alone there's a good chance I'm having a solo dance party.

"Come on, Rain!" I shouted, and in my giddiness grabbed his hand and ran after Dillion and Kayla.

Momentarily I thought I should let go, what kind of message would that give him? But did it even matter?

I had been ignoring all the emotional tension between us the last four days, and now they were at the forefront of my mind. As we zigzagged our way through the sea of people, the music pouring from the bars got louder and livelier. Alcohol fueled nearly every partygoer, us included. Tongues loosened, smiles broadened, and feet skipped and tapped to the rhythm of the street. Laughs floated freely through the air, happily mingling with the smoke rising from cigarettes, vape mods, joints, and open windows. I was wrapped up in the buzzing energy of the night. I felt light and elevated. My final shred of resistance was quickly fading away, giving into the previously hidden longing I had for Rain.

I can't hurt Trevor like this, cautioned my inner voice, but the reminder was muffled. Like I was trying to hear it through a closed door.

What he doesn't know won't hurt him.... For the past few months this thought had been a mere whisper. Now it was reverberating throughout my mind.

I won't do it, I strained to think. *But why are you still holding his hand, then?* demanded the voice in my head.

I didn't have an answer. Not because I didn't know. But because I didn't want to admit to myself what I really wanted.

"This is it!"

Abruptly I was snapped out of my interior monologue by Kayla exclaiming that we had arrived.

"This is a pretty shady entrance... even for a bar," Dillion cautioned.

"Come on, do you remember where we are? It's New Orleans. If it didn't look shady, people wouldn't go inside," Kayla joked.

I was with Dillion on this one. The door blended in with the wall, so we had to move into a shadow to see where the light fell on a faint outline of a rectangle. The paint was faded and peeling, and there was a hole where I assumed a handle once was. A handwritten sign had been secured with bright orange duct tape above the handle hole that read "Just push it open, Stupid"

"Oh look, at least they're friendly," I said sarcastically.

Kayla ignored our protests and proceeded inside. I wasn't about to stay out by myself, so grudgingly I followed.

The foyer was dimly lit, and it smelled slightly like a wet dog wearing cheap cologne.

From around the corner stepped a very tall, eccentric-looking man. He was dapperly dressed head-to-toe in a bright orange three-piece suit dotted with black jack-o'-lanterns.

"IDs please," he said as he held out his hand. His fingernails were painted to match his suit.

The four of us pulled out our licenses to prove we were over twenty-one (we all were of course, but I'm pretty sure everyone still thought I was fifteen.)

After a quick glance at our cards, he tossed them back, then reached a long arm around the corner to unclip a chain that was blocking the doorway to the rest of the parlor.

This certainly wasn't like any karaoke bar I'd ever been to. Why was it so dark? And why did that guy smirk when he let us in?

My questions were quickly answered.

Beyond the foyer the room opened into a small lounge. It was arranged with five round tables and an assortment of big half-moon shaped chairs all set in front of a large stage. The stage was elevated and took up about 50 percent of the room. On the platform were three poles with three very naked women dancing and gyrating up and down them.

"Oh... My... God," I heard Dillion whisper.

"Awe, fuck it anyway...," Kayla mumbled to herself.

With a helpless look she turned to us. "I'm sorry, guys; I took you to the wrong place. The karaoke bar is another street down. This is a strip club."

"Well, I kind of assumed as much." Rain chuckled.

"We can't just leave, though," Kayla said. "We have to stay for at least one dance, otherwise it'll be obvious we fucked up. Plus, it'd be rude."

I didn't really understand why we had to stay but didn't complain. The four of us found seats at a booth to the right of the stage, Rain pulled his seat closer to mine so the armrests were touching. I was sitting on the very edge, trying to touch as little of the chair with my body as possible. My hands were resting on my knee when he reached over and placed his palm on top of them.

I could hear the voice in my head coming back, but it was faint, lost in the alcohol-clouded maze of conflicting thoughts. I brought my gaze up to meet his. Even in the pale light of this Bourbon Street strip club, I could see the flecks of green in his eyes.

He leaned in closer so that we were mere inches from each other, my heart was pounding in my ears.

"Rain, I—"

But his lips stopped me from finishing my sentence.

Just like that he was kissing me. For a split second, less than that even, I considered pulling back. But in that moment, I remembered the first day I saw him. I remembered the intense foreshadowing I had felt when our eyes met. Everything was suddenly coming full circle. The pressure of temptation melted away, and I kissed him back, shattering every wall between us like glass. He cupped my face in his hands, then gently moved his fingers down my neck, along my spine, to rest on my thigh. I, likewise, ran a hand through is sandy hair, and with the other grabbed his waist, slipping my pinky finger through the belt loop of his jeans to pull him closer.

We were unashamedly making out between these two oversized chairs, oblivious to anything else, completely lost in our own world when Dillion chimed in with, "Oooooh shit. Yep, they're gonna fuck."

Hearing his friend, Rain looked up from me to punch Dillion in the arm. Then they both laughed, and we all agreed it was time to get outta there.

Giggling at the predicament we had gotten ourselves into, the four of us slipped out of the strip club back onto the street.

Stepping off the curb however, I took an extra big stride to avoid a puddle of unidentified glittery liquid that was filling a pothole and tripped. Rain caught me and Dillion rolled his eyes. I held on to Rain's arm to steady myself, then willingly took his hand and once again followed Kayla to the karaoke bar. This time we ended up where we were supposed to be.

The bar was decorated with every manor of spooky paraphernalia. Orange lights were strung up like spiderwebs at every corner. Fog machines camouflaged as gargoyles sat on each side of the stage and every bartender was dressed as their own version of Dracula. The mood for a stellar Halloween Party had been expertly set.

We weaved our way through the sea of people till we found an open spot on the floor and fell into sync with the rest of the crowd, jumping and dancing to the music bumping from the speakers. We cheered for every soul who got up on stage to sing, no matter their level of drunkenness. After a few rounds of tequila shots, Kayla was pulling me up on the stage to take part in a dance off. Joined by six other partygoers, we had to mimic the karaoke hosts moves and were then judged by the crowd on which one of us was the best dancer. In a "last man standing" kind of fashion the contest continued until all but one was eliminated.

Five songs later I was the only dancer left on the stage.

"Holy shit, you wooooon!" I could hear Kayla whooping and hollering below.

The DJ stopped the music and the host held up my hand as if I had claimed victory of a boxing match.

"Everyone give a round of applause for tonight's karaoke dance-off winner! You killed it, baby!" he boomed into the microphone.

The crowd cheered, and I took a dramatic bow. Then hopped off the stage to rejoin my friends.

"That was amazing!" Rain shouted over the music.

Then for a second time, his lips were on mine, only now he was more confident. With both one hand on the small of my back, the other on the base of my neck he pulled my body against his. I wrapped my arms around him and again was kissing Rain like there was nothing else in the world that mattered.

"Get a room!" someone yelled from behind.

We turned to see it was Dillion (no surprise). He was leaning against the bar chuckling to himself while holding Kayla's hand as she twirled in a circle around him. (she was heavily intoxicated at this point, so her circle was more of a bean shape, but you get the picture)

The night carried on like a dream. We danced to our heart's content. I was never more than an arm's length away from Rain. Eventually we heard the Hosts voice come through the speakers.

"Laaaaast caaaaaaaall! Time for you drunken fools to GET OUT."

We scrambled out with the rest of the club. Our feet were aching, and our brows glistened with sweat, but we were happy, so very happy. Back on the street, we watched as a parade of street performers scattered into a star formation and put on a show right there in the middle of the crowded pavement. It was quite the spectacle, complete with boom box, vibrant leotard body suits, and ingenious choreography. It felt nearly hypnotizing. A circle grew around the performers, pressing the audience closer together. I held tight to Rain's hand. This was organized chaos at its finest. I looked at my friends and smiled, completely in awe at the beautiful execution of it all.

This was one of those moments where time slowed to a standstill. For once I wasn't thinking about what was morally right and what wasn't. I felt zero guilt about kissing Rain. I felt only a tantalizing rush of rebellion. I was living in the moment, and for now the moment was perfect. I didn't worry about the consequence tomorrow might bring. The joy I had was genuine, the night was alive, and I secretly wished it would never end.

Why can't my life stay as it is now? The voice was back. With my buzz wearing off, it had found its way out of the cluttered mind maze.

Like all perfect nights, this one came to a close quicker than I would have liked.

~...~...~

Chapter 17

About Last Night…

Dillion and Kayla stumbled into their bedroom and were passed out before their heads hit the pillow.

Rain and I stood for a moment in the kitchen. The single bulb in the ceiling fan cast long shadows across his face, making his expression oddly mysterious. I tried to think of something clever to say, but my recent sobriety and need for sleep were rapidly overcoming the ability to form a full sentence. Rain broke the silence.

"Hey, thanks for a great night, Nat."

I could feel my cheeks blushing. "It really was, wasn't it?" I said, and I meant it.

If I didn't walk away then, I knew I wouldn't be sleeping alone, and wasn't sure I wanted things to escalate that quickly with him, or if I wanted them to escalate at all. This wasn't just a one-night-stand kind of deal, where you don't have to remember your lover's name the next morning (it's polite if you do, but if not, no judgment.) this was a best friend, a relationship I was scared to damage..

I kissed his forehead, then walked down the hall to my makeshift couch-bed. Slowly, reality began to return. Every footstep sounded too loud and the high from the night was completely gone, leaving me with a low ringing in my ears. My throat was parched, and water suddenly sounded like a good idea. Turning into the hall bathroom to get a drink, I flipped on the light, turned on the sink and cupped my hands under the faucet. I took three large gulps before splashing the cold water on my face and scrubbed until I'd gotten off all the residual grime left from the festivities.

Eyes still closed I grabbed the hand towel to pat my face dry, but before looking up into the mirror, I just stood, elbows on the counter, my face buried in the towel. All I could see was Rain—that spark in his emerald eyes, his sandy red hair glowing in the neon lights, and his smile... his blissfully happy smile that never left him after that first kiss.

Then another face came to mind, a face I could picture so clearly, whose dark brown eyes I saw perfectly when I closed my own. I saw Trevor. Back at our apartment, probably asleep, waiting for me to come home in two days.

What if he knows... what if he had seen us tonight? I thought miserably. *He would be devastated...heartbroken.*

"Oh my God, Natalie," I said out loud. *Now look what you've done.* The voices in my head were at full blast now, practically screaming.

Abruptly I looked up at my reflection in the mirror. I didn't like who I saw.

With a big sigh, I dropped my gaze back down, flipped the lights off and walked to the couch. What if Trevor never finds out? Did I really have that little of a guilty conscience to keep this from him?

No. If anything I wished I had less of one. I knew there was no way I couldn't tell Trevor. This night would eat away at me from the inside out until he knew the truth.

Maybe if I told him part of it, I thought. *He doesn't really need to know all the details, right?*

Then I began to worry he might leave me if I was 100 percent honest with him, and the thought of that made me want to cry.

"Fuck you for thinking you could have the bests of both worlds," I said to my feet.

Then my head hit the pillow and I was out.

~...~...~

Why is the sun so bright? I thought.

Slowly I sat up, squinting with just one eye open to try and diffuse the late morning sunlight streaming through the window. My phone on the floor blinked up the time: 10:25 A.M.

Scanning the room, I spotted my boots laying in the doorway with the twisted plastic grenade bottle stuck inside the left one. The red straw rolled out onto the floor. Rain had bought me that drink. I smiled at the thought.

Rain. Last night. Strip Clubs. Karaoke. Trevor. Oh God.... My sleepy smile turned grim. Everything from the night before came rushing back. (It was like when your friends play a prank of dumping ice water over your head after being the first to fall asleep at a middle school sleepover.)

A small part of me hoped that the night on Bourbon Street had just been a wildly vivid dream. But the bottle, the smudged 21+ stamp on the back of my hand, and the dull pounding in my head convinced me otherwise.

I couldn't think about everything just yet, otherwise I'd curl up in a ball on the floor and never leave this room. I'd deal with it later. Priority number one was just getting up and out the door.

Today was our last in Louisiana. We were leaving that morning, with Rain driving back to Colorado in his new car, and me headed back to Illinois. I still had a week of time off, so I was going home for a bit, plus Trevor and I had another friend's wedding to attend.

As I gathered my things into my duffel bag. I hoped that maybe Rain would see last night as just a onetime thing. Kind of like "what happens in Vegas stays in Vegas."

We could go back to just being good friends as if nothing happened. Trevor would never find out, and I could keep my boyfriend without losing a best friend.

It's possible, right? I laughed out loud at this. Shouldering my packed duffel, I walked out into the kitchen where Dillion and Rain were sipping coffee. Kayla was still in the bathroom. Apparently, her hangover was worse than the rest of us.

"Good morning!" Rain greeted me cheerfully. "I made you some coffee."

"Thanks." I smiled back and took the steaming mug. The warmth from the coffee felt soothing on my increasing headache.

"Well, I have to be getting to work," Dillion mumbled. "I'll go get Kayla so she can say goodbye to you two."

Please don't leave, I thought to myself.

I didn't know what to say if Rain and I were left alone. Luckily Dillion wasn't gone long enough for the silence to become awkward. He returned with a very disheveled Kayla. Her hair was in a tangled knot at the top of her head, smeared eye shadow could be seen behind her glasses, and her face was rather pale.

I suppressed a laugh. But Kayla just waved her hand at me and exhaled.

"Oh, let it out, I know I look like a hot funkin' mess."

We all chuckled; I admired her ever-present humor. After hugs were given, goodbyes said, and promises to stop by next time we were in the area, Rain and I left our friends' home to the cars waiting outside. I tossed my bag in the back, took a deep breath and turned to face Rain. He walked from around his driver side door, so we were standing toe-to-toe.

"Now what?" he asked.

"I don't know," I said. "I think I just need some time."

It was a cliché thing to say, I know. But it was all I could think of.

"I don't want to share you," Rain said softly.

I don't know what I was hoping he would say, but it wasn't that.

"Oh... um...." I struggled for words

"I really like you, Natalie. I have for a long time; you've known that. And now I just want you to be mine, nobody else's," he said firmly.

"Oh, Rain... I can't just jump into another relationship. I mean. I *AM* still with Trevor. You know that," I told him.

"Well, do you want to be?" he demanded

"I... I... I honestly don't know right now. Which was partially true. Right then I wasn't sure of anything. My ability to feel emotions had been left on pause.

"Just please give me some time, Rain," I asked.

"I can give you time. But promise me you aren't going to be with anyone else until I see you again back in Colorado. Promise me you aren't going to blow me off. Because if this is not going to go anywhere, if you don't really want to be with me, just tell me now so I can start to deal with it. I don't want any bullshit."

The seriousness in his eyes rendered me immobilized. I couldn't look away.

"I'm sorry," I said. "I wish I had a better answer for you, but really I just don't know."

The pause that followed seemed to last for ages. Eventually, his gaze softened, and he reached out to hug me. I felt him sigh and lean into my shoulder.

"I've just had so much shitty luck my whole life, Natalie. It's been a goddamn fight since day one. No one has ever listened or cared about me like you do. Seriously, you really are my one best friend."

I was grateful Rain couldn't see my face, or the single tear that was sliding down it. I held him tighter. He then continued. "And I know that's a lot to ask of you... if anything, though, just promise you won't hurt me."

Without hesitation I said, "I promise."

As soon as those words left my mouth, I stepped back from our embrace, and kissed him one last time, soft and slowly like all goodbye kisses should be. I did it more for him than for me.

"I don't want you to go," he said as I got into the driver seat.

"I have to, Rain."

"I know…," he murmured glumly.

"I'll let you know when I'm home safe and sound," I said with one hand on the door handle.

"Okay, I'll do the same, have a safe drive back,"

With that he stepped back from my car, I closed the door, and we both drove off down the road. When we came to the intersection for the interstate, Rain turned left, and I went straight. I glanced up into my rearview mirror and saw him grin. Once he was out of sight, I couldn't shake the feeling that that was the last time he would smile at me.

~…~…~

Chapter 18
About Heartbreak

Hours later I was pulling into the driveway of my parents' house. Not too long ago, I had been in the exact same spot, only this time I was alone, and instead of stars, the sky was shrouded in a thick blanket of clouds.

"Well, that's fitting," I muttered to myself about the sky overhead.

It was an unusually warm sixty-five degrees outside. I stood for a moment, my unmatched socked feet on the driveway rock and leaned against the SCION. How many times throughout the years had I pulled up in the dark outside this house? Too many to count. Numerous outings with friends, returning from bonfires with the lingering smell of woodsmoke on my jacket. I would quietly tiptoe up the porch steps in the first hours of morning, avoiding the board that squeaked. Then I'd pull open the screen door and hold it until it closed to avoid a slam. Immediately I would slip my shoes off and slide down the hallway trying not to pick my feet up too much. Finally, I would step over the sensor light in the hallway so it wouldn't turn on and shine under my parents' bedroom door.

I smiled thinking about those nights. No matter how quiet I stepped, or how softly I shut my bedroom door, Mom would always know exactly what time I returned home. I swear, you could run a train through that house and my dad wouldn't stir, but a mouse could sneeze in the crawlspace, and my mother would be up searching for the intruder.

The garage code was the same four digits from when I was in high school. Leaving all my bags in the car to deal with later, I walked into the garage and opened the door leading into the house. The kitchen lights were off except for the one over the sink. Quietly I set my keys on the counter and slipped down the hallway to my old room. Sure enough, the door to my parents' room was cracked open. Carefully I pulled till it clicked shut.

The next morning, as promised, I texted Rain to let him know I was home. He had been texting and snapchatting me periodically through his drive, but this was my first response to any of them.

Immediately I saw his text bubble appear at the bottom left corner of my phone. Seconds later "good morning beautiful" appeared on my screen.

Normally, I would feel butterflies at such a text, but this time I felt like I'd swallowed a rock, a large one too.

I heard a door open followed by footsteps down the hall. Then my mom appeared in the kitchen doorway. Usually I could tell her anything, and she would miraculously have the best advice. But I wasn't ready to re-tell the whole story just yet. So, when she asked how the trip was, I began with the drive to Florida and focused on the fun parts like the beach, buying Rain's car, meeting his mom, and the Halloween bonfire. Nothing about Bourbon Street.

But as if she could read my mind, she asked me, "So how are things between you and Rain now?"

Damn she knows, I thought. *How does she ALWAYS know?!?*

"Ummm... fine," I lied.

Mom gave me a look that said, "Okay, I don't believe you, but I'm not going to pry."

"Well, it's fine for him at least," I added.

"What do you mean? Did something happen on the trip?" she asked.

"Sort of," I replied

I paused for a moment and stared blankly into the mug of coffee I was holding. Whether they're told up front or not, Moms usually figure out the true story eventually. In the end I gave up and spilled everything, all the details. From the night at the bonfire at our old apartment, to the strip club, to my promise not to hurt Rain and all the mixed-up feelings that were now knotted in a tangled mess in my gut.

By the time I finished talking, my throat was dry and I wished I had some Baileys for my coffee.

Mother was mulling over my confession. I walked over to the table and sat down, then stared wide eyed, waiting for this woman to reveal the answer to my problems.

"Well, Natalie. Who do you want to be with?" she asked.

"Trevor." I was surprised at how quickly his name left my mouth.

"Okay, then be with Trevor, but not without total honesty. If you want to have a healthy relationship, my dear, you need to tell him what happened between you and Rain, and hope he forgives you."

She made sure I was listening before continuing.

"More importantly, you need to tell Rain the truth too. The longer you continue to lead him on, the harder the fall is going to be for him when he hits the ground. You really shouldn't have promised you wouldn't hurt him."

This wasn't what I wanted to hear.

"I know! But what else was I supposed to say? He really is one of my best friends, and I don't want to lose him…," I said desperately.

"Then you shouldn't have kissed him," my mom said plainly.

"Ugh… but I wanted that too… at the time anyway." I could feel my temper start to rise. "God!" I shouted in frustration. "Rain's going to hate me, and it'll all be my fault. Why do people have to fall in love with me?!"

My last words came out more conceited than I intended. But it was basically true.

My mom chuckled, uncrossed her legs and crossed them again in the other direction.

"Oh, honey… you were foolish to think that. All your life you've been a fast friend to everyone, especially those no one else will give a chance to. Your kind heart and optimism has drawn many good people to you, but you must learn when to draw the line at just friendship. You've teetered on it before, but this time you've jumped waaaay over it."

It was difficult for me to hear all this. But I knew she was right. Trevor would arrive tomorrow for our friend's wedding. I had talked to him about as much as I had talked to Rain since I'd gotten home. Seeing him in person, I knew I wouldn't be able to keep a secret for long. But I needed to talk to Rain first, that way I would at least have something more conclusive to tell Trevor. It was just a matter of finding the right words in the right moment.

The following day I drove over to Trevor's parents'. He was outside working on the Escape and looked up from under the hood when he heard my car pulling into the driveway. Brushing his hands on his pants, he adjusted his ballcap and strode towards me. After slamming the door of my car shut, I skipped over and leapt into his outstretched arms. He hugged me tightly but let go sooner than usual. I brushed that off though, and asked how his drive back was, what he'd been up to, and how work had been going, which carried into the afternoon. I rode with him to pick up his tux for the wedding, stopped for ice cream at our favorite spot, and ended the evening with dinner at his parents. Usually I would have stayed late into the night, but after a whole day together without saying anything about Rain, I was getting anxious. Looking at his loving, innocent face was becoming torture. I was afraid if I didn't leave soon, I'd impulsively blurt out the wrong thing at the wrong time. So, with an abrupt goodbye, and some lame excuse for why I couldn't stay, I ran out the door.

Today had shown me more clearly how much I needed Trevor. Despite his flaws and sometimes lack in communication, he was loyal through and through. I could trust him wholeheartedly. I had selfishly taken him for granted. I realized I had the kind of guy all my single friends wanted, even the ones in a relationship complained to me about their boyfriends and how they wished they had someone like Trevor. I had a guy who loved me for being myself. Right now, I didn't deserve him, but I was going to do my best to change that.

When I got home, thankfully the house was empty, no distractions. Gritting my teeth, I grabbed my phone and went out onto the back deck. It was a cool evening, and the moon was in a perfect crescent. The house had started to feel claustrophobic, plus whenever I was stressed, being outside always made me feel better.

Opening my messages, I saw many from Rain. The farther down I read the farther my heart sank. What had started with "good morning beautiful" ended with "Why are you avoiding me? Don't leave me in the dark." Right before I pressed the call button my phone dinged with another message. This one read: "Okay. Just tell me the truth so I can start accepting whatever this is."

It was now or never.

He picked up on the first ring.

"Hey, Natalie," he said.

"Hey."

"What's going on with you?" he asked.

I took a deep breath, then started unraveling the truth.

"I'm sorry, Rain, I've been trying to think of the right way to tell you for the last day now. But the truth of it all is that I do like you, and I do have feelings for you, but it's just happening at the wrong time. Being home I've realized how good Trevor is for me. I'm sorry I had to pull you in, and I know I'm breaking my promise; I know I'm hurting you right now, but there won't ever be anything more between us. I let my emotions rule my decisions and that was stupid. I like you a lot, Rain, but I love Trevor and I always will."

At first, he didn't say anything. From his end of the phone line I heard a crackling sound, like someone was holding a beer can and crushing it in their hand. Then he retorted with, "Yeah. That's why you cheated on him, right? I thought you were different. You're just like every other manipulator. Thanks for reminding me never to trust anyone. You really fucked up my head. Have a nice life. I feel sorry for Trevor."

I didn't hesitate.

"All right, first of all, the reason I ever cheated on Trevor was because I guess I have a problem with hurting the people I care about. I hate it. I always have let things go too far. I know I've fucked it up. It's a wonder Trevor's still with me. But it's not my fault your life has been a shit show. I've tried so hard not to hurt you, and to be the person you can open up to cause I know you've never had that. You did mean something to me. I was never trying to play you, but if that's what you think, then fine."

I took a big inhale and carried on, talking faster.

"Your temper can get the better of you; you're out of control sometimes, and that scares me, Rain. That's why I'm so cautious about what I say because I don't want you to lose it and just leave. God, this feels like a breakup. I'm sorry I fucked up your head, and I'm sorry it's come to this, but I am different from the rest because I do care, and I will have a nice life. Guaranteed."

The other end of the line was silent. I thought maybe he had hung up. But then he spoke again, a little quieter, with long pauses between his sentences.

"It's not your fault my life's a shit show... I know that... but you gave me hope, girl... just to crush it... whatever... I should have known. I'm the stupid one.... Why, though? Why end like this? All I ever did was return your kindness."

I softened my voice too.

"I know; that's what makes this so difficult. I didn't intend to lead you on. There were moments when I thought what life might be like with you. You were there for me and listened when Trevor didn't. The farther I got from him the closer I got to you. I was avoiding one problem by creating another. I should have been honest as soon as I knew you and I couldn't be more than friends. But I liked the attention. Believe me, I'm disgusted with myself… nothing has been harder to say. I'm so sorry, Rain, and that's the truth.

"Yeah, I'm sorry too," he said, his voice calm and steady. "It's going to take a while to pick my heart up from this one. Especially after you walked all over it. But I'm glad I know now. This is for the best. I couldn't trust you wholeheartedly anyway. Wouldn't want to be in your shoes. Must be hard living the honest life of a liar."

Then the line went dead.

That last blow hit hard. It was done, though. Rain knew the truth of how I felt. I couldn't recall a time I had felt more alone. Not only did I break a heart, I broke a friendship, smashed it to pieces. Letting my phone slip from my grasp, I crumpled down against the side of the house and hugged my knees against my chest. An owl cried somewhere in the distant tree line. I didn't try to stop the tears. There on that clear night, under the crescent moon, I cried into my folded arms, and allowed myself to be engulfed by the ash and smoke of the bridge I'd just burned.

~…~…~

Chapter 19
About the Truth

"I hope the rain clears up before this afternoon. Walking through mud in heels never works well for bridesmaids."

I nodded in acknowledgment of my mother sitting across from me at the table. A slow drizzle was falling from the clouds. Three days had passed since my falling out with Rain, and for the most part, I was feeling okay. Not great, but not terrible. I still hadn't filled Trevor in on everything, but that would change tonight. It was getting almost unbearable holding it in, but I didn't want to trouble him during the preparation for his best friend's wedding, he was the best man after all. So, I had decided to wait until after the ceremony was over. When the reception was underway, speeches had been said, and he was in good spirits I would pull him to the side and ask if we could talk. He was also leaving back to Colorado the next day, so I didn't have a lot of options for time.

Fortunately, the moment came without my doing. The dreary drizzle had stopped before the ceremony was to start. The sun came out, and the ground wasn't too soft for heels. It turned into a beautiful afternoon. Since Trevor was in the wedding party, I joined a table with a circle of my old friends. Time passed in merriment until it was time for speeches and first dances. Eyes were dabbed and cameras flashed as the bride and groom rocked back and forth on the dance floor in their first dance as husband and wife.

Another slow song followed, and the rest of the groomsmen and bridesmaids joined the newlyweds. Trevor walked over to where I was sitting and held out his hand.

"Can I have this dance?" he asked raising one eyebrow.

"Of course, you can."

He pulled me close to him, and hand-in-hand we swayed and twirled around the floor amongst the other couples.

"You know, we haven't slow danced very much together," he said

"I know… we should make more time for that," I replied.

"So, we will. We should make more time for a lot of things…."

I rested my head on his shoulder.

"I've missed you, Natalie," he whispered into my ear.

"I've missed you too," I whispered back

As the last few notes of the song faded out, and the upbeat whimsical intro of the Cha Cha Slide began, Trevor stepped back and took my hand.

"It's getting a little warm in here," he commented. "Would you like to step outside with me?"

"Um, yeah sure that sounds perfect actually," I said.

He led me just outside the party tent to the concrete ledge bordering the landscape.

He sat down on the ledge and patted the spot next to him.

I scooted over to him, and he put his hand on my leg. I placed mine on top of his and waited to see if he had a reason for bringing me out here. Trevor wasn't one to leave a party for serious conversations, so I knew that he probably wanted to tell me something.

"Is everything okay?" I asked.

"Well, not exactly," he replied.

I waited.

"Being home and seeing you all dressed up, and dancing with you just now… I'm just really happy you're my girlfriend. I really don't know what I would do without you. I know I haven't said that in a while, and I'm sorry. I should tell you more often how much you mean to me."

Wow, this wasn't at all how I planned this night to go. I was speechless for a moment.

"Oh… Trevor, thank you for saying that, but you don't need to feel sorry for—"

"Yes, I do," he said, cutting me off.

"The past couple months I've been distant and cold to you. I haven't been a good boyfriend, and there's no excuse other than I just didn't want to talk about anything, even when we had the chance. I've been keeping all my feelings inside, and I'm sorry.

"Stop." I held up my hand.

"I can't let you keep going, Trevor. I'm the one who should be apologizing, not you. When it comes to things being kept inside, I'm just as much to blame, and I don't ever want to hear you say that you are a bad boyfriend. Every relationship has some sort of communication deficiency; it's natural. But you are loyal and trustworthy and truthful, and I cannot say the same for myself...."

"What do you mean? I can trust you... can't I?" he asked nervously.

"I wish ...." I sighed loudly and mentally prepared myself for the following conversation.

"I kissed Rain when we were in New Orleans."

"What...?" I saw the color drain from his face a little.

"Well, technically he kissed me, but it doesn't matter. I kissed him back. I could have said no, I could have pushed him away, but I didn't. I wanted the attention, and I didn't want to hurt him. I wasn't thinking about you and then stupidly thought you wouldn't find out. Once I came to my senses, I panicked and thought you would leave me, which I wouldn't blame you if you did. You don't deserve any of this, and I'm so so sorry.

I took a breath and waited for him to process my confession. He let go of my hand.

"Why didn't you tell me sooner?" he asked, barely opening his mouth to talk.

"I couldn't... I had to tell Rain first. But I told him we won't ever be more than friends, that I led him on, and that I wished I didn't hurt him like I did. Now I'm pretty sure he'll never speak to me again, which is probably for the best."

Trevor looked past me to the end of the stone ledge.

"Wow... I, um... wish I knew about all this. You sure did a good job of keeping your cool. Maybe if I had paid closer attention, I would have noticed something was wrong...."

He tapped his heel against the side of the wall, then stood up and started pacing.

"Damn it! I should have told you I had a bad feeling about that trip," he shouted. "God... I'm so bad at this talking-about-your-feelings thing. None of this would have happened if I would have just opened my goddamm mouth!"

"Okay, seriously, stop apologizing." I was standing up now too. "Did you hear what I just said? You should be angry; you should be upset with me."

"Well, I'm definitely not happy about it," he said.

I studied the ground.

"You know with everything that's happened these past few weeks, my mind's been emotionally overwhelmed. I tried so hard to make everyone happy and especially hard not to hurt those I care about, but that's exactly what happened. Only now I've seriously learned my lesson that I just have to let some problems go, and it's not my job to fix them. I've been selfish. I've taken your trust and loyalty for granted. You've turned my life into something more than I ever thought it would be. I've learned things about myself I never could have if it wasn't for you. I wish it hadn't taken something like this for me to realize I don't want to see you go. But now I'm just rambling…. I hope…maybe… with time you can forgive me… because I've never been sorrier.

"Natalie, I already forgive you," he said, looking up at me again. "I'm just glad you told me. What's done is done. It's going to take some time to process everything, though. I can forgive you, but I don't know if I can trust you for a while.

"…yeah," I replied. "I wouldn't trust me either, but you can trust that this won't happen again."

Trevor nodded and started fidgeting with a low-hanging tree branch.

"Do you want me to leave," I asked.

He looked up at me. His eyes looked tired.

"I never wanted you to leave. I know I can be a bit distracted, but even though you're a real handful sometimes… I'll always want you to be close to me. You're my girl. You know I love you."

Scotty (the groom) spotted Trevor and motioned for him to come inside. Trevor held a pointer finger up to his friend and turned back to me.

"I think I should rejoin the party; Scotty looks like he needs another drink. I could use one too; what do you say?" he asked me.

"Actually, I think I'm going to head home, but could I have a hug before you go back in?"

Without a word, Trevor pulled me into a tight hug and held me close to him until I could feel his heart beating. "We'll get through this," he said.

And with that he went back to his buddy's in the reception tent. I stayed outside and watched my boyfriend joke and laugh with the other groomsmen.

I knew that this wasn't the end of the Rain-Natalie-Trevor triangle, but the worst was over. All that was left was time for healing. I walked back to my car in the parking lot. I could have stayed but really didn't have the energy to force a smile anymore. My mental marathon was on its last leg, and right now I just wanted to go home.

~...~...~

Chapter 20
About Healing

Back in our little mountain town, I returned to work at Ranch House. It was back to the grind double time with the approaching holiday season. I skied as much as I could during the mornings and even some backcountry rides at night with Trevor and Brandon. The sport had really turned from a hobby to a passion for me. Flying down groomed slopes at high speeds, weaving through ashy barked Aspens, I liked to pretend I was a snow leopard. Sleek and elusive silently gliding over fresh fallen snow, the solitary sound being snowflakes bouncing off my jacket. Sometimes I would stop, free of worry, close my eyes and imagine I was the only soul for miles and miles. This was my mountian, this was my home.

Trevor too, returned to work in his usual amicable manner, staying true to his positive attitude. I asked him several times if he wanted to talk about anything, and if he really was okay. But every time he assured me that he was, that there wasn't anything on his mind and I should stop worrying.

I tried, but I just couldn't believe that was totally true. I refrained from asking too much though, and began to accept that maybe he really did get over it that quickly.

Unfortunately, I was right. Trevor really wasn't fine, and his feelings eventually came to the surface. He just needed some stronger provoking, and it happened on the night of the employee Christmas party at Devil's Thumb Ranch.

I was looking forward to seeing my fellow employees all dressed up and taking part in the holiday festivities. The vast reception barn had been turned into a Christmas Wonderland. Garland and holly lined the doorframes and windows. Red and white petaled poinsettias sat at the center of every table, and white icicle lights hung in delicate streams from the ceiling, casting a magical glow over the open dance hall. In the center of the room was a very extravagant dinner spread complete with a roast beef carving station. Everything from flambéed sweet potatoes to a three-tiered Christmas cookie tower sat waiting before us, begging to be consumed.

Trevor and I found seats and waited for the welcome announcements to finish so dinner could begin. We both were in fine spirits until I spotted a familiar face leaning against the wine bar at the far end of the hall. Dressed in black slacks and a deep purple dress shirt, Rain sipped a glass of Pinot Noir while twirling a candy cane around his index and middle finger. He glanced up from his glass and for a moment we locked eyes.

Ah shit, I thought, and quickly looked away, hoping Trevor hadn't noticed my sudden change in demeanor. Of course, he was here. He worked for the same place that we did after all. Why wouldn't he come to the Christmas party?

I can be an adult about this, I told myself. *I'm not going to let Rain ruin this night.*

I also wasn't about to let him keep me from getting a drink. Standing up a little too abruptly, I told Trevor I was going to get some wine and headed over to the bar. It was on a rare occasion that my coworkers saw me dressed in attire other than a chef's coat or having my hair in more than just a ponytail with a black uniform toque. I was wearing a dark brown and amber sweater dress with charcoal gray tights and matching Calvin Klein boots. My nails were painted a deep red to match my earrings and I had brushed on a hint of eye shadow. My hair fell down my back in loose curls, and I noticed some of my fellow employees doing a double take when they realized it was me. I looked good tonight, and I knew it. With a strut I approached the bar and asked the bartender for a merlot. I didn't look, but I could feel Rain's gaze on me. This near proximity was the closest we had been since we said our goodbyes in New Orleans. Daintily I took the glass from the bartender's outstretched hand, flashed him a smile and turned sharply making sure to whip my hair slightly in Rain's direction. I knew he was watching me walk away, and I couldn't help wonder what he was thinking. When I sat back down at the table next to Trevor, I was nervously aware of how fast my heart was racing.

After dinner had been served, tables cleared, and awards handed out, it was finally time for the music to start. The DJ turned up the party and soon the entire room was alive. I danced with my friends to every song, thoroughly enjoying myself. By the seventh song, I needed to cool off, so, while Trevor went to refill his water, I stepped out into the coat hall for some fresh air. A few others were there doing the same, I grabbed a cup and was headed back to Trevor by the water fountain when I felt a tap on my arm.

"Natalie," I heard a voice say from behind.

I turned around, and there was Rain, empty wine glass still in hand.

"Oh… hey," I said.

"Um… how are you?" he asked.

"I'm doing pretty good actually," I replied. He set his glass down on a nearby table.

"Listen, would you want to go somewhere more private for just a little bit? I thought maybe we could talk in person… you know because we haven't since you left me in Louisiana. Maybe get a little more closure on everything."

Once again, I was unprepared for this.

Don't do it, Natalie, the voice in my head cautioned.

I could see Trevor through the doorway, his back was towards me, and he was standing next to the table talking with a group of friends. He surely wouldn't notice if I snuck away for a moment.

"I guess I could do that," I heard myself say.

"Thank you." Rain sighed and motioned for me to follow.

He led me down to the empty first floor common room of the resort. Only a few hall lights were on, but a fire burned brightly under the hearth. The entrance door was locked so no one could come in from the outside. There were no guests staying in this part of the resort for the purpose of the Christmas party, so we were very much alone.

Rain stood in front of the fireplace watching the flames throw flickering shadows across the floor. I sat down on the edge of an armchair and waited for him to speak. When he didn't say anything, though, I thought I should just go back, and started to stand up when he said.

"I'm sorry, Nat."

"For what?" I asked.

"For everything. I knew you were with Trevor, but I had wanted you all to myself for so long I just didn't care anymore. I thought you wouldn't want to be with a screwup like me. Then, for a minute, I thought you might, but I shouldn't have been so foolish."

"Rain, thank you, but I'm just as much to blame as you if not more. I ruined a friendship between us. As much as I'd like it to be, we cannot have that back, you know that."

"I know." He sighed again and crossed his arms. "That's not why I asked you down here. I just wanted to apologize to you in person. Especially for saying those things I did over the phone. You are not like everyone else; you really did care about me, and I wish it didn't have to end. That night in New Orleans was great while it lasted."

"Yeah, it was," I told him. "But you're not the only one who said things they didn't mean. I was just angry and sad. I cried myself to sleep that night…."

"I did too," he said quietly.

"You're not a screwup, Rain. You are just a good guy who bad things have happened too, and you are a fighter; don't ever change that."

"Thanks." He smiled a little. "I'll be all right. I've gotten this far."

I looked down at the hardwood floor and then stood up from the armrest I was sitting on.

"I think I should go back upstairs now," I said.

"Yeah, I guess you're right; thanks for talking with me, though. I feel a lot better now."

"You're welcome; I do too." As I turned to head back up, he stopped me once more.

"Um… would it be too much to ask for one more hug?"

I had been very conscious of the distance between us since we had gotten down here. I was making certain not to get too close.

"No, that wouldn't be too much," I answered.

In three strides he closed the gap between us and put his arms around me. His hand rested on my waist and he softly whispered, "You look absolutely gorgeous tonight."

And as soon as he said it, he broke our embrace and stepped back in front of the fire. I turned again to walk up the steps, and he didn't stop me this time.

~…~…~

I like to think that as I walked out of sight, Rain smiled. I hope he really did feel better because it did no good to live in a world of what-ifs.

He was meant to be in my life for a short period of time, just as I was supposed to be in his. Like a meteor that burns bright until it falls to earth and simply is gone. I wished him the best, but it was time for moving on.

Back upstairs I immediately scanned the room for Trevor. I hadn't realized how long I had been gone, and he was nowhere in sight.

"Damn it," I mumbled under my breath and started to panic.

If someone saw me leave with Rain and told Trevor I would be in serious trouble.

I tried calling him with no answer. I tried again, still nothing. Sometimes service was bad in the Reception Barn (ironic right?), so I stepped outside, but there still was no answer. People had begun to leave the party now. Through the emptying parking lot, I could see his Escape was still there. At least he hadn't left.

Anyone leaving had to come through the main entrance, so I sat outside on the ledge and waited. After thirty minutes, there were few people left, and Trevor had still not answered any of my phone calls. I was starting to get worried and was also starting to get very cold. Finally, once his was the only car left, he came strolling down the sidewalk, his hands in his pockets no signs of concern or need to hurry at all.

"Oh my God where have you been!" I shouted. "I've been waiting and looking for you for over an hour!"

"Where have I been?" he said, appalled. "I could ask you the same."

"I was talking to Rain. He wanted to apologize in person, and I thought it was a good idea. Nothing happened. I swear we were just talking. I'm sorry I didn't realize the time."

"I know," he said. "After you left, I looked for you, but Vic told me you left with him, so I went to talk to David so I wouldn't come find you and kill him."

"You wouldn't do that," I scoffed.

"Try me babe, I would," he retorted.

"You could have called me; I had my phone. I thought you had left with someone else," I said.

"Oh, I thought about it, but clearly you'd rather spend your night with Rain than with me."

"Trevor where is this coming from?" I asked. "You said you were fine. I promise I told you everything about him and I."

"Yeah, well I'm not," he said, and with that stomped off toward the Escape.

Quickly I hopped after him trying to avoid slipping on the snow with heeled boots on.

"Trevor!" I yelled. He didn't turn. He just got into the driver's seat and started the engine. I climbed in the passenger side and slammed the door shut.

"Well, do you want to talk now," I demanded, slightly out of breath and shivering.

He said nothing.

"Trevor, do not tell me that there isn't something bothering you."

Still silence. He started to pull away. Now I was really annoyed.

"Come on! Why do you insist on keeping your opinions pent up? It doesn't make you a bigger man. I know you've got to be upset, for God's sake let it out!"

Ding, that was it. I struck a nerve.

"OKAY!" he shouted and punched the steering wheel. "I'M FURIOUS!"

Like a ticking time bomb that just hit zero, he exploded.

"You want me to let it out?!? I'LL LET IT OUT! I have been on the brink of an outburst ever since you came home! I can't even think about Rain without seeing red! He's lucky I didn't destroy him when I saw him tonight!"

"Then why didn't you tell me any of this?!" I pleaded with him. "Why did you keep saying that you were fine?!"

"Because I didn't want to talk to you!!" he shouted.

"Oh... well I—" I started to say, but he cut me off.

"I'm sorry, Natalie, but I really just couldn't open up to you right away after you hurt me like that. What if you were in my position? What would you do huh?!"

"I would at least talk to you! Not lie about how I felt!" I said.

"Oh, do you really want to bring up dishonesty right now?!" he yelled sarcastically.

Trevor hardly ever spoke like this, especially towards me. I wanted him to speak his mind, but I also wasn't ready for this verbal beating.

"No, I'm... I'm sorry, I just want us to be okay again; what do you want me to say? Tell me, please," I asked him helplessly.

"I don't know what you should say, Natalie. There's nothing you can say to change what happened. I thought you were better than this."

Now I was fighting tears. Trevor had never come close to making me cry, but I guess there's a first for everything.

"I thought I was too…," I sniffled. "Believe me you can't make me feel worse than I already do. A part of me was afraid you would be gone when I got home from Illinois."

"I thought about it," he said.

"Why did you stay, then?" I asked.

I think seeing me so upset made him calm down, and he lowered his voice again.

"Because I thought about what I would do or where I would go. And no matter how angry I got or how tempting leaving sounded, when I seriously thought it out, I knew I wouldn't be very happy in the long run without you. I can survive on thrill and adrenaline and be content roaming from ski town to ski town. But damn it, girl, you have my heart, and I don't think I could get it back if I tried."

I was choking back sobs at this point and had to concentrate on taking deep breaths before speaking again.

"Well, I'm glad you didn't leave," I said, looking out the window.

We didn't say any more until we pulled up in front of the apartment. I didn't open the door right away. I looked down at my feet and rubbed my eyes, which were finally dry again. Without a glance in my direction, Trevor reached over and rested his hand on top of mine and sighed loudly.

"I'm sorry for yelling at you like that. I didn't mean to get that upset," he said calmly.

"It's fine, you have every reason to be," I said back.

He looked at me then and said, "Let's just focus on moving forward, and promise not to hide anything from each other, good or bad from now on. I know it's going to take some effort to completely heal from all this, but at least we can start by being honest."

"I would like that," I replied.

"Ready to go inside?" he asked.

I nodded, and together we walked back into our studio apartment. Before he got to the bedroom, Trevor turned and hugged me. I rested my head on his shoulder, and we stood there in the hallway just holding each other for the first time in a while.

Without letting go, he said softly, "Hey, what do you say this summer we go somewhere new."

I grinned and lifted my head up to see his face.

"Okay, where do you have in mind?" I asked

"How 'bout Alaska?"

I laughed out loud.

"Alaska? Sure. I mean I've only dreamt of going there since I was little."

"Really?! Cause I've been thinking about that a lot actually," he said eagerly.

"If you're serious, I'm serious; why not? It wouldn't surprise anyone back home. They thought we were crazy for moving to Colorado. Alaska would just be a little farther," I said.

We both were laughing now.

"Want to do some job searching tomorrow?" I suggested.

"Definitely," he agreed.

Chapter 21
About Alaska

With the commitment of new adventure planning, we crawled into bed. It had been a long night and sleep came swiftly and soundly. The next morning Trevor had to be awake early for work. I got up to see him off, and after a quick cup of coffee and a kiss goodbye, he was out the door.

I had the day off and while it would probably be a great day for skiing, I wanted nothing more than to sit at home curled up in front of the fireplace and finish reading the book I had started three months ago. No need for any socializing today.

I prepped a second pot of coffee, and while the grounds were brewing, I searched for my favorite mug. It had a pocket for your hands to go in and stay warm. But when I opened the cabinet, I spotted another mug in the back that had been left in the apartment by the previous owner. We had never moved it and I'd forgotten about it. Reaching back and arching my arm slightly to avoid knocking the other mugs, I picked it up and saw that it had a black and white silhouette of a mountain range on it. In white lettering around the rim it had the iconic John Muir phrase "the mountains are calling, and I must go."

I chuckled to myself. I hadn't always related to that phrase, but I certainly did now. This made me remember what Trevor and I had said last night about going to Alaska.

The machine hissed as the final drops fell into the pot. With a new energy at the thought of an Alaskan summer, I poured a steaming mug of coffee, nestled into the couch, and opened my laptop to begin job hunting.

At first, I didn't know where to start. Usually when I did this, I had a particular job in mind. All I knew was that I wanted to be working outside and not in the kitchen for a change. Not that I disliked the chef life, but if we were going to make this big of a step why not use it as an opportunity for something totally different? The outdoors was where I felt most at home, and if I could get a job primarily outside, and in Alaska, I would be set up for the best summer of my life.

I scrolled through pages of openings, read many job descriptions and filtered through with keywords like *guide, hiking, backpacking*, etc.

Before I knew it, three hours had come and gone and my hand-warming mug sat empty. My searching was not without progress, though. I had done a little research into multiple outdoor touring companies that piqued my interest, and by lunchtime I had applied to a few different positions. One was for a hiking guide in Denali, another for a wilderness educator in Kodiak, and a third was for a bicycle tour guide in Skagway.

Satisfied with my morning, I closed the laptop and picked up my book that I had been neglecting for too long. Trevor would be home soon, and I couldn't wait to show him where I had applied to.

A week passed with no reply from any of the companies. Another week and still nothing. Then on December 26, the day after Christmas I had an email in my inbox from the bicycle company in Skagway. They wanted to set up a phone interview and were requesting a time that worked best for me. I quickly replied with a few time slots, and soon they responded with tomorrow at 10:00 A.M. Mountain Time.

"Yes, thank you, I look forward to hearing from you!" I immediately typed back.

The next day at 9:57 A.M., I was nervously waiting next to my cell phone. I would sit on the couch, become too restless, stand up, pace back and forth, then look at the time to realize only a minute had passed.

The closer it got to 10:00 A.M. the more anxious I became. At 10:01 I stood up to look out the window for the 100th time that day. I noticed the sun was disappearing behind heavy, low hanging clouds. I thought we must be in for some more snow.

My daydream was interrupted by my blaring ringtone. I jumped, the caller ID said Haines, Alaska. I inhaled sharply, then exhaled all the nerves out and answered the call.

"Hello, this is Natalie," I greeted.

"Hi, Natalie, this is Becky with Sockeye Cycles. How are you doing this morning?"

From that point forward, conversation came easily. The interview was more laid-back than I had anticipated. She asked me questions regarding travel, bike riding experience, public speaking skills, and general "get to know you" things. It was only supposed to last thirty minutes, but an hour later we were still on the phone. I was in the middle of telling Becky a story about a bike race in Illinois when I heard another phone ring in the background.

"Oh, my goodness is that the time?" She exclaimed. "Well, Natalie, I'm sorry to have to cut you off, but I have more phone calls I need to make before lunch."

"Yeah, no worries," I replied. I had lost track of the time too.

"All right, well it has been such a pleasure getting to talk to you, usually we do a Skype interview following the phone one, but I believe I've gotten all the information I need. If we decide you are a good fit for our team this summer, we will send you an offer letter via email. So, watch your inbox."

"Okay I will, thanks so much, Becky, have a good day."

Then the call was over. Once again, I was alone with the couch and my nerves. Only now they had switched from anxious to excited. I hoped I had said all the right things, but the more I tried to replay the interview in my head the more my words seemed to run together and escape recollection. It didn't matter, though. Besides, Becky seemed genuinely pleased with all my answers, now all I had to do was wait.

~...~...~

I didn't have to wait long. Later that night around 9:30 P.M. (7:30 P.M. Alaska time). I heard the ding from my phone notifying me of the new email.

Nonchalantly I swiped the home screen over to the Gmail app, and when I saw the subject line, I did a double take. In bold letters it read **Job Offer Letter**

I clicked on it and started reading. The first line said:

Hello Natalie, on behalf of Sockeye Cycle Co. we would like to offer you the position of bicycle tour guide with our company this summer. We believe you would make a great addition to our team.

I read those first two sentences three times before making it through the entire email. I had two days to give them my answer.

"Hoooooly smokes!" I exclaimed.

I couldn't believe it. Trevor hadn't even gotten home from work yet and already I had a job in Alaska.

I read the email one more time. Then typed out "Thank you so much, 100 percent yes!" and hit Send.

Maybe that was too enthusiastic. I shouldn't have made that all caps, I thought to myself. Oh, well.

With a satisfied sigh I fell backwards onto the couch from my perch on the armrest. Brushing the curls out of my face, I looked up and out the window to see snowflakes falling in the light of the streetlamps. Since the interview I had kept busy with chores and such inside and hadn't noticed how much fresh snow had fallen.

Quickly I hopped up from the couch, pulled open the front door and gasped. From the edge of the small porch all the way out to the tiny headlights on the highway was nothing but white. The roads around our little suburb were completely covered and untouched, making it look as though from the tips of my toes to Highway 40 was just one big glorious snow meadow. And the flakes were still falling.

"Ah ha ha!" I shouted. A rush of cold air blew in as I shut the door, sending a wave of goosebumps down my arms. Frantically I looked around for my snow boots, found them, tried to put them on the wrong feet, tried again, grabbed my coat, zipped it up halfway, and then ran out into the winter wonderland. For a brief moment, I just stood in all that fresh powder. It came up nearly to the top of my boots. The snowy blanket muffled everything, the loudest sound the pitter-patter of snowflakes landing on the roof above. A surge of joy grew inside me. The kind that swells up in your chest making you stand just a little taller, forcing its way into the biggest smile until finally I couldn't hold it in any longer. I broke the peaceful silence with a happy holler and took off running through the drifts, kicking the snow into the air, making snowballs and tossing them as high as I could. I was acting like a child. It was glorious. The open landscape, freshly snow covered, gave an illusion that the ground surrounding me was flat, but I knew where the dips and bumps were hidden, so with a leap of faith I jumped from the edge of the driveway into the ditch and landed with a muffled "umph" into a pile of soft icy crystals. Giggling I lay in this makeshift nest allowing the cold flakes to land and melt on my flushed cheeks.

Part of me felt guilty for disrupting the untouched pristine snow. It just looked so beautiful, especially at night with the surface sparkling in the pale glow of the streetlamps, but in all honesty, I had absolutely no regrets.

Fresh powder like this was meant for playing, and play I did. I romped and jumped and skipped through the snow until I had just enough energy to make it back to the front porch. Contently exhausted I plopped myself down on the cooler sitting outside the door and leaned my head back against the side of the building. I closed my eyes and my mind drifted back to when I was a little girl kneeling beside my bed at night praying for snow. For as long as I could remember, from the time I could talk, whenever my family would say a nightly prayer I would ask for snow. Even if it was the end of July, I would still pray for snow that following winter. Now it felt like all those prayers were getting answered.

There never was a heavy snowfall where I grew up in southern Illinois, but out here in the Rocky Mountains of Colorado I had enough to fill all of my wildest dreams. Turns out not all prayers are answered right away, sometimes you have to wait until the moment is right. You may not know it then, but you'll know when the time comes, and it's usually when you least expect it. Kind of like receiving an anonymous gift you never knew you needed. This was one of those moments, unexpected, but so much better than I ever thought it could be.

In this wonderful, unpredictable, and everchanging novel that was my life, Alaska was a blank page. A new adventure. Untouched and open like the view directly in front of me tonight. I didn't know what awaited in the chapters ahead, I didn't know what words would be written, and I didn't know what kind of new characters would be introduced. What I did know, was that I held the pen in my hand, and I unequivocally could not wait to find out.

THE END